ON CUE

MANAGING ANXIETY, INVITING EXCELLENCE

RON THOMPSON, PSYCHOLOGIST-MASTER

MASTERFUL
LIFE-PERFORMANCE

Published by Masterful Life-Performance Press
576 Lightening Ridge Road
Plainfield, Vermont 05667
www.masterfullifeperformance.com

Cover Art by Patricia Lyon-Surrey, "Autumn in Black & White"

ISBN Number 978-0-692-26842-1

CONTENTS

INTRODUCTION

ON CUE
Managing Anxiety, Inviting Excellence

I walked slowly across the tough browning Bermuda grass of Theodore Judah Elementary in East Sacramento. Gazing down at my dusty US Keds, I contemplated what I would do with my life. I'd just turned nine and it was time to choose. My life lay before me and it was an important life, not to be wasted on the trivial, but to be directed toward some purpose equal to its importance. I decided to become a peacemaker. It seemed to me that peace was what the world needed more than anything, and my role would be to contribute. This choice came to me quickly and easily, as did the answer to my next introspective question: by what means would I carry out my peacemaking?

I had recently begun to take private trumpet lessons from Bill Peron, whom I considered a magician on the instrument. Music making, specifically trumpet playing, would be my path. What could inspire peacemaking better than music? Now that this was all settled, I could go find some friends and a football and play keep-away.

It's been sixty-three years since that day. Little has changed with regard to my core values. The other day I found myself wondering if they still make high-top US Keds. My feet felt so springy in those shoes. My sixty-three year peacemaking path has given me much springy living as a husband, father, grandfather, professional classical trumpeter, trumpet teacher, musician, electrical engineer, business administrator and counselor.

This book is a sharing of insights harvested from the life experience of many people. I have organized these insights into an approach to human performance which I have named Masterful Life-Performance. The book is an exchange of letters between myself and a fictitious person, Evelyn, who represents many of the people with whom I have had the privilege to work.

I've just been asked to perform the *Adagio* from *Telemann's Concerto In D* for the Christmas Eve service at the old white Universalist Church, an agent of peace in Barre, Vermont. Telemann must have been experiencing a place of peace similar to that experienced by a soaring eagle, as he wrote this high, solo trumpet music. There are four high D's in this celestial piece. These notes are at the top of my range, and my lifestyle leaves little resource for practicing trumpet and strengthening my trumpet lip. The piece requires all the endurance I can muster, and my being in a state of peak performance. On Christmas Eve, a festival celebrating the birth of a man many call The Prince of Peace, I will be way out on the tree branch of performance risk, in an effort to give the congregation a few moments of flowing peacefulness.

The process by which I will invite my soaring peak performance on Telemann's *Adagio* is the process I now share with you in these pages.

Peace to you,
Ron Thompson
December 2014

LETTER 1

Dear Ron,

Over the years we've had lots of late night talks, right? Talking about this or that, mostly about the challenges of my life: my trials at work, dealing with my fellow surgeons (Oh my, the egos!), my dog training hobby, and even my Teddy Bear collecting.

Now it's time to talk about what really concerns me and what really confuses me. I'm talking about the anxiety that I experience daily, especially when I want something badly, like the successful outcome of a surgery I've performed, professional recognition for a presentation at a medical conference, validation for writing a journal article, or even doing a good job showing my dogs at a dog show. The damned anxiety knocks me off balance. It's so detrimental and stupid.

My self-condemnation is the pits when outcomes don't meet my expectations, or when I avoid even trying something due to my anxiety.

I do a lot of stuff... lots of accomplishment... but there's a whole universe of opportunities that I have avoided because of my fear. And resilience? Sure I come back. But it takes a long time. Way longer than I want it to take.

I know I'm bright. That's not the issue. I have tons of talent. I know I have advanced clinical skills and that I can write well, think logically and communicate clearly. My health and athletic skills are terrific. I have lots of dear friends. I used to act in musicals and plays. I love art, music and theater. But occasionally when I go to do something socially important to me, anxiety raises its ugly head... and hurts my performance... and stifles my creativity... and keeps me from expressing myself fully, from being myself. Geez!

Okay, Ron, there I've spilled it all out, or at least some of it. I know you are not going to put me down.

Tell me what you know about human performance, with special attention to performance anxiety. How about we exchange letters? Writing is best for me, because it allows me plenty of time to think about the issues... my issues... and your responses.

Give it to me straight... nothing sugar-coated. You hear my truth, and I hear your truth. I imagine you address this issue often, with clients involved in all kinds of performance, from golf to orchestra auditions. I know peak performance and performance anxiety are your special interests because of your life as a trumpet player.

Let's set up this question-and-answer dialogue with a sense of mutual curiosity and caring. No time line for the project. When we start, we start. When we finish, we finish. Are you up for it?

Standing by.

Evelyn

LETTER 2

Dear Evelyn,

You're on.

Through the years I've heard the emotional pain embedded in your stories, an emotional pain that I believe to be common, perhaps even universal, in the human condition. The pain of performance anxiety is most certainly familiar to me and has provided a genesis for interest and passion in my personal and professional lives. I believe that you and I can maintain an open and honest discussion of our emotional experiences and associated world views. I look forward to this deepening our relationship and as a valuable, even noble, exercise. Thanks for your trust.

So, we're off! Send me a question.

Ron

LETTER 3

Dear Ron,

Yay! I thought you would go for it. It just seemed like your kind of thing. Let's see... a question?

Why do I get so anxious about almost all of the things I do involving other people? Examples are my medical conference presentations, entertaining guest VIP's, playing golf with colleagues, and even showing my dogs at dog shows. I get more nervous about showing my dogs than when I do surgery. It boggles my mind.

Evelyn

LETTER 4

Dear Evelyn,

A general answer to your question about why you feel anxious in the several settings you mentioned is that anxiety is an emotional signal that you are not getting your needs met. Three emotions signal that needs are not being met. They are anger, sadness and anxiety. All three are associated with negative emotional tension and all three are responses to actual or projected personal loss.

Sadness is the emotional signal associated with past loss. Anxiety is associated with anticipated future loss. Anger, which can be directed externally or internally, is generated when we link our emotional pain to specific causes through the use, or implied use, of the word "should." I "should" have done better. They "should" have responded more enthusiastically. "Should" is an interesting word-concept that I will discuss with you in greater depth in another letter. For now, please link its use with the emotion of anger, and think of anger, and its less intense form, irritation, as a sign of emotional pain.

The needs of which I speak are universal human needs, those that are essential to human existence and common to everyone. We have physical needs, such as nutrition, exercise, sleep and shelter. We have social needs, such as social belonging, social acceptance and social contribution. We have need for emotional peace through the experience of beauty, order and harmony. We have mental needs, such as the stimulation associated with curiosity. We also have spiritual needs associated with experiencing loving attitudes, especially toward self. Examples are self-trust, self-acceptance, and self-forgiveness. For an excellent discussion of needs, I refer you to Marshall Rosenberg's book, *Nonviolent Communication: A Language of Life*, in which he shows how communication can be formed and used to identify unmet needs and reduce emotional pain.

If we gain an understanding of which of our needs are at risk for being unmet, we are in a stronger position to moderate our anxiety. Because anxiety is associated with the anticipation of personal loss, it is helpful to name the anticipated loss and to create internal and external strategies for reducing vulnerability. Through the years I have assembled a collection of observations, ideas and practices that I call Masterful Life–Performance (ML-P). ML-P is the master plan strategy that I use in my personal and professional lives and I will be sharing it with you.

Evelyn, it's time to hear from you. Is there anything I've said that begs for clarification or that leads you to another question?

Ron

LETTER 5

Dear Ron,

Hmmm, these are some really new ideas. I have always thought of performing as a display of learned technical skill. My instructors never addressed the more philosophical or psychological aspects of performance. For them (and me!), it was all about mastering and demonstrating a skill set. Performance was nothing more than this. Kind of one-dimensional. But you are emphasizing universal human needs and their relationship to emotions, especially anxiety. Also, it sounds like you're emphasizing the importance of social connection and attitude toward self. Do I have that right? And if so, then just how important is skill mastery?

Evelyn

LETTER 6

Dear Evelyn,

Thanks for bringing up the subject of skill mastery. My training as a classical musician also emphasized technical skill mastery. The message from my trumpet teachers was that the only path to confidence is through absolute technical mastery. They did not talk directly about confidence (or lack thereof) in performance. Their total emphasis was on how the music was to be played and the achievement of technical mastery. In my youthful ignorance, I accepted this notion that technical mastery was the only path to confidence, and I took it to heart. By age nineteen I had spent over 10,000 hours behind the trumpet. If I messed something up in performance, even because of nerves, it was because I had not practiced enough. I went back to the practice room and practiced more, often into the night. My approach was one-dimensional: Practice, practice, practice.

What I have come to understand is that technical mastery is crucially important to Masterful Performance, but that it is only half of the process. The other half is composed of a social component and an attitudinal component. But I am getting slightly ahead of myself. Let's go back to technical mastery.

By the time I had finished two years at Juilliard, having spent the 10,000 hours at the trumpet and studied with two world-class teachers, I had few technical shortcomings. However, I was not confident in all performances. I can remember assisting in the senior recital of my friend and colleague Charlie Schlueter, who later became the Principal Trumpet of the Boston Symphony Orchestra. Armando Ghitalla, then the Assistant Principal of the Boston Symphony, was in the audience. My concern about impressing him, or more accurately, not making a mistake in front of him, made me feel overly anxious in that performance. This was true even though I had high technical mastery of the music. I underperformed slightly in that recital. *I was a trumpet player performing, rather than a performer playing trumpet.*

However I was determined to continue performing, even though I was plagued by excess anxiety and what seemed to be the randomness of peak performance experiences.

Two milestone performances supported what I began to call The Performance Puzzle: The easy stuff is hard, and the hard stuff is easy. Or more precisely: Sometimes the technically easy performances are emotionally difficult and the technically difficult performances are played with relative emotional ease.

The first milestone occurred when I was nineteen. I was performing a Mozart symphony as Second Chair Trumpet in the National Symphony Orchestra in Washington, D.C. Mozart trumpet parts, especially second trumpet parts, consist mainly of simple bugle-like calls. No big deal technically. The setting was Constitution Hall, a massive concert hall and the home of the NSO. A threatening, emotionally distant conductor and a discriminating audience of two thousand were out there. In this particular performance my musical support consisted of a highly competent, refined major symphony orchestra. Even with this highly disciplined team and an easy trumpet part before me, I felt extreme anxiety. My thought focus was distracted, my heart pounded and my throat was constricted. The trumpet is a wind instrument. Playing it with a constricted throat is like watering the garden with a crimped hose. I was emotionally disabled, unable to direct the bell of my trumpet any higher than the music stand directly before me. Now, remember, the commanding timbre of a symphonic trumpet is prominent in the fabric of the symphonic sound. It cannot disappear, but to disappear was all that I wanted. I desperately wanted out. I was in such a state of discomfort that all subtle grace and coordination in how I held the instrument to my lips was lost. A helpless, irritated confusion engulfed me. How could something this technically easy, over which I had obvious technical mastery, be so overwhelmingly difficult? My technique-only performance paradigm was in a state of painful disintegration. Another, more complex performance paradigm was evolving as it moved, ever so slowly, down its birthing canal.

At that point in my career I had played in about 1,000 public performances. Years later, at about the 2,000 mark, another milestone performance occurred. This time the setting was Fiesta Night in Santa Barbara, California. From the second-story balcony of the massive Moorish County Courthouse, I performed the technically virtuosic Raphael Mendez arrangement of *La Virgen de la Macharena (The Prayer of the Bullfighter)*. That evening several thousand watched the spotlighted balcony. The trumpet solo had taken years of practice to master. My musical support system for that performance: a marimba. From under a gold-filigreed black sombrero, I presented a flawless, rapid-fire, no-sweat *La Virgen*.

After that performance, my mind flashed back to the Second Trumpet Mozart Symphony experience. As I made the comparison, my technical mastery paradigm was shattered. Technical difficulty and technical mastery clearly were not the only determiners of whether I was anxious or confident in my performance. It had to be the audience.

I began to notice that I played with varying degrees of emotional tension in different settings and with different audiences, as I gave many performances in the Santa Barbara area. I realized that my performances at the Old Mission Santa Barbara were much more comfortable than my Santa Barbara Symphony performances. I enjoyed playing for the church congregations at the Old Mission much more than for the audiences at the symphony concerts in the Arlington Theater. I explained this to myself by thinking that I was audience-sensitive. Again, I had absolute technical mastery of the music in both settings. I reasoned that the primary difference was the audience.

I began to blame the audience for my discomfort. The damned audience was causing my emotional pain in performance. I began to hate the damned audience. It was not just the damned audience now – it was the God-damned audience. I began to use this hatred to help alleviate my anxiety. I noticed if I became angry on stage, my anxiety decreased and my performance improved. The problem was that I could not sustain the anger. Typically, after the intermission,

I couldn't keep sufficiently mad, and some of the anxiety returned. Also during this time I began a trial of Inderal, a beta-blocker medication commonly used by musicians to reduce performance anxiety. I did not like the idea of routinely relying on medication to perform, and I noticed an unmistakable dullness in my performance experience.

During a particular Santa Barbara Symphony concert I decided to investigate the "God-damned audience." There was no trumpet part on one of the compositions, so I took a vacant seat in the balcony and began my watch of the audience. Most of the people were older and gray-haired. Many were attentive, but as the music rippled out from the distant stage some heads became bowed. A short snore emanated from a seat close to mine, prompting a smile across my face. An older gentleman to my right was tending the needs of an adult male who appeared to have a developmental disability. As I viewed my empty Principal Trumpet chair, so small and distant on the stage, the thought crossed my mind that this audience bore no resemblance to my "God-damned audience," no resemblance whatsoever. A light went on in my mind. The audience out here was not my Real Audience. In truth, my Real Audience was in my head. *It was within me.*

Evelyn, does this begin to clarify the relative importance of technical mastery? Those 10,000 hours behind the trumpet were absolutely crucial, however Masterful Performance necessitates an in-depth understanding of Real Audience.

Prior to the Santa Barbara Symphony concert described above, I experienced a glimmering awareness of my own interior Real Audience. It came during a performance anxiety workshop given by the now legendary Eloise Ristad. *Purple Fairy Boots*, which I have included in this letter, is the story of that experience.

Ron

Purple Fairy Boots

I can't believe this. She's wearing purple fairy boots. You know, like the ones that Peter Pan wears. We're going to spend the whole day with her? Learning about music performance? But then again, she has a sparkle about her that is intriguing to me.

My friend Val, a remarkable musician, had told me not to miss Eloise Ristad's performance workshop. "She's in her sixties, a former piano teacher, from Boulder, Colorado, with an imagination that doesn't stop. She's helped hundreds of musicians and written a terrific book on overcoming stage fright, *A Soprano On Her Head*... that's right, the title is *A Soprano On Her Head*. It's from a student of hers, a singer who learned to overcome her stage fright by singing upside down nestled under Eloise's grand piano. Don't worry, Ron. Some of the best classical musicians in the country work with her. She's really great... you'll see."

It's unsettling, being here in this stark university classroom, with all these musician-strangers. I've never spoken with anyone about my trumpet performance anxiety, let alone paid money for a workshop. I'm glad Val's here. And then there's Eloise. Almost immediately her playful inquisitiveness becomes a source of curiosity and reassurance to me. She calls us each by name as she takes out some homemade beanbags, pairing us up, one beanbag per pair. She asks us to toss the beanbag into our partner's outstretched hand. We throw back and forth at her signals. Then she asks us to close our eyes and do the toss. It's remarkable how many of the pairs catch the beanbag. She says it all has to do with imagination, curiosity and focus.

She teaches us that anxiety and curiosity do not co-exist; that curiosity neutralizes and dissolves anxiety.

One after the other, she works with each of us, the whole day, tirelessly.

My turn comes. I play the cornet solo from Berlioz's *Harold In Italy*, with a sudden flashback to when, at age 18, I nervously performed it in the student orchestra at Tanglewood, the summer music camp coached by members of the Boston Symphony Orchestra. I played that concert with one slight performance blemish, the significance of which didn't even qualify it as a mistake. But after that concert, I returned to my dorm room and beat myself up emotionally for not playing it perfectly. My way was to beat myself up into perfection, and then practice more. It had worked quite well. I had overcome every technical challenge I had faced and won every audition in which I had entered.

Yet, on my bed in the Tanglewood dorm, I quietly wept.

Now, here at this workshop, Eloise was about to initiate me into a life-long interior process of dissolving my perfectionism and my fear-based life perspective, and replacing them with a love-based perspective that honors my attraction to excellence. She began by introducing me to my internal critical and self-condemning patterns of thought.

When I finished the Berlioz for Eloise and took the trumpet from my lips, she asked me a question. "Ron, who is your judge?"

My father's face flashed in my mind's eye.

Dad, a man whom I admired above all others, my childhood god, my protector, my rock of stability, the author and example of my personal standards of moral and intellectual excellence, the competent one, my definition of a real man.

This man whose own father had died of tuberculosis in 1912, just as Dad was emerging from diapers. Dad, the man who loved and supported me from a distance, who never got in my way, and yet who was never free enough within himself to demonstrate a convincing appreciation for my musical accomplishment and passion.

The ghost-face of my father revealed an insight hidden just beyond my conscious awareness. My perfectionism was driven by my fear of losing his respect.

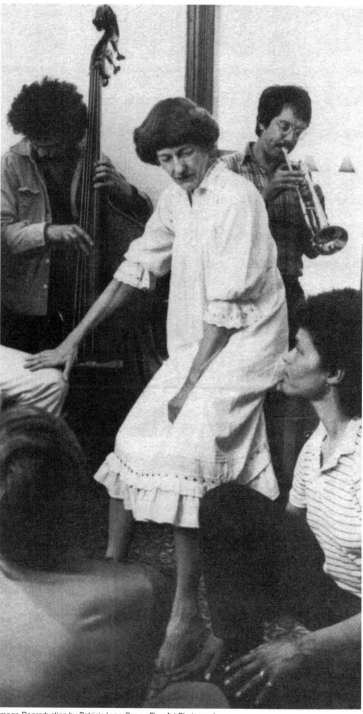

LETTER 7

Ron,

The skill mastery jives with my experience. That part is perfectly clear. What I can't quite get my mind around is your emphasis on Real Audience. In the story, I guess you are telling me that your Real Audience was your father. Even though you held him in very high regard, still he was a powerful judging presence in your mind. So to you he was an audience. Evidently he was also your (harsh?) judge.

Eloise really nailed you when she asked you to name your judges. This is getting interesting. A bit heady and abstract, but interesting.

I need more clarification. I get the shift from audience-out-there to audience-in-here, but talk more about what seems to be really two audiences. What about the real people out there? What about them?

Also, it's mind-boggling that you did so many performances, especially with anxiety always threatening. And you were a teenager for a lot of it. I guess the peak performances must have more than balanced out the painful ones. Anyway, you kept going.

I guess I keep going too. We just plow through, don't we?

It's fascinating that you observed and analyzed your performance process so carefully. You used your own experience as your laboratory and tried all kinds of strategies. Forgive me, but I liked the God-damned audience strategy the best. Hilarious on one level, but poignant on another.

We have something in common. Both you and I have felt lots of anxiety and feelings of helplessness. It's not fun! I hate not being strong and I hate being so vulnerable.

When I'm in that painful state, I have no trouble generating and spreading blame. I spray it around like DDT. On all manner of things: myself mostly, my parents, God, my training, the weather. You name it.

I seem to have no trouble getting in my own way. There's an old saying about being your own worst enemy. Quite true for me.

So, please keep talking to me about this, especially clarifying your ideas about audience. And maybe you can throw in a story about a particular performance. I like stories.

Evelyn

LETTER 8

Evelyn,

I will definitely talk more about the concept of Real Audience, and the idea of two audiences. Before I do, I want to acknowledge the depth of emotional and physical pain that we as evolving performers can experience. Like you said, performance can be accompanied by strong, painful feelings, and a sense of abject helplessness. Indeed, there are times when performance demands a burning sense of compartmentalized focus, in spite of the pain. In orchestra circles it is called playing hurt.

You asked for a story. Here are two. One is from my trumpet performance experience, entitled *A Gift*. The other, *No Big Deal*, illustrates how emotionally intense performance can be, and makes a comparison with a life-threatening incident. Please let me know how, and if, they resonate with you.

Ron

A Gift

The trumpet case I've been carrying has been an extension of my right arm for years. At seventeen, I hardly notice the weight of it. At night, it is at the foot of my bed. You see, my trumpet is my best friend.

The brass sign reads Juilliard School of Music. Just inside the building a smaller sign directs me to the Admissions Office. My acceptance letter says for me to be here Now. As I go in, a middle-aged woman of warmth and refinement asks me if she can be of help.

"Yes... I am Ronald Thompson. I'm here for my trumpet instructor placement audition."

"Ronald, please take the elevator to the second floor, turn right to room 214. We have a pianist accompanist who is expecting you."

I didn't expect an accompanist. I certainly do not want to waste my chops rehearsing while he learns his part. I'm nervous enough without having to deal with that.

The incessant sharp pain between my legs is really distracting. It's been there since morning. I first noticed it when I got on the bus to come up here. It hurts especially when I walk.

"Ronald?"

"Yes."

"I'm Emanuel, your accompanist. May I have the music please?"

"Thank you."

I take my trumpet-friend out of its case. I've spent thousands of hours with my Meha French Besson. My whole teen life. The lacquer that used to protect its shininess is all but gone. My sweat has eaten it away.

My trumpet carries the fragrance of musty valve oil, which is a curious mix of odor and aroma. In several places on the instrument there are subtle indentations; wear areas, worn precisely where my hands grasp, and unconsciously rub, long practice hour after long practice hour. The three fingering valves are totally loose and lightning fast. They have learned to travel up and down their little casings, following the hammer-like biases of my over-practiced fingers. If someone else tries to play my horn, the valves are likely to stick.

Emanuel plays the Haydn with me – right the first time. Our brief rehearsal is over.

God, that pain between my legs is really something! I popped two boils on my back last night. I bet it's another boil. And right square where the bottom of my stem attaches to the rest of me. Oh man, does that hurt!

There are several men in the room, all seated behind a long, extended, mahogany-veneered table.

One stands.

"Ronald Thompson?"

"Yes."

"I'm Roger Smith. The Brass Faculty welcomes you to Juilliard, and to your trumpet instructor placement audition."

"What have you prepared for us today?"

"The Haydn Trumpet Concerto, Sir."

"Please proceed."

I'm flying through the Haydn, as if on auto-pilot. Thank God for the pain between my legs. It is a welcome distraction from my insecure thinking – my intense desire for their approval and the opportunity to study with my trumpet hero, William Vacchiano, Principal with the New York Philharmonic. In the past, my mouth has gone dry at important moments such as this, erasing any technical control, and leaving me embarrassed and humiliated.

In trumpet performance there are no soft mistakes.

Thank God for the pain. A blessed distraction. A gift.

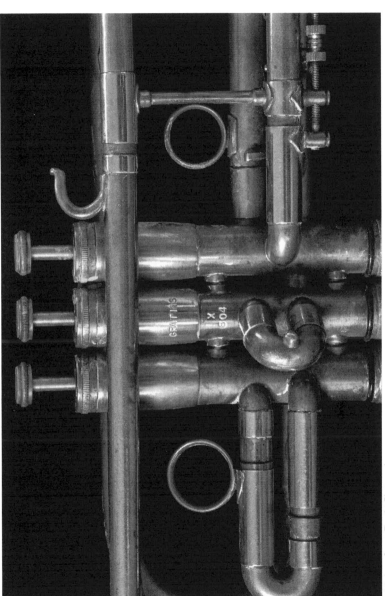

No Big Deal

The snow is falling just enough to cover the quarter-inch of ice on the unpaved, unsanded, remote country road. Slowly coming down the hill my Toyota 4-Runner picks up a bit of unwanted speed. I gently touch the brakes. Now it is all drama. A fishtail, a 180-degree reversal in direction, no control, a sideways slide toward and over the edge, down a ten-foot embankment, a roll-over down into the waiting ravine, an abrupt crash stop. I'm upside-down, pinned inside the car. The tree that stopped the roll-over is just outside the driver's window. The windshield is shattered but intact. I'm hanging upside-down against my seatbelt, bleeding a lot from the top of my head. I feel my scalp. The laceration I feel there is longer than my hand is wide. My hand is covered with blood. The damned wound just keeps bleeding. And all down my new Barbour barn coat, my favorite piece of clothing. I try my blood-covered cell phone. No reception. The driver's door is jammed shut by the tree. The passenger's door is blocked by the ravine wall. There's no way to punch through the windshield. Am I going to bleed to death here, trapped in this driver's seat? What a stupid, senseless way to die!

I hear a welcome knock at the passenger's window. A man in overalls and a green flannel shirt asks me how I'm doing. I tell him: "I'm Okay." He says to turn around. He'll try to open the back hatch. It opens with a jerk as I unbuckle and crawl along the ceiling, out to freedom. As I crawl I pick up part of an old beach towel and press it to my bleeding head. I inch up the side of the ravine on my hands and knees to the road.

A lady has stopped to help. She keeps trying to get me to sit down. I don't want to sit down. I want to walk around and stand while I wait for the ambulance. She keeps pestering me to sit. I tell her that this is No Big Deal, and that I want to handle it my way. I have the realization that this condition is not a big deal to me, and that it feels very familiar. The racing heart, the hyper-vigilance, the extreme focus, the regulation of the deep breathing. It's exactly like the experience I've had many times in my professional music performance life.

Now she's really on my case. I don't want to sit, and certainly not in her car. My bloody face looks right at her. I say: "This may not make any sense to you. I'm a professional trumpet player. This is just like playing a difficult solo in a concert. I'm all right." All I get back is a blank stare.

The EMT guy in the ambulance had a different opinion after he took my blood pressure. "Mr. Thompson, you're okay, but you're in shock. We'll have you at the ER shortly."

As it turned out, my head did not even need stitches. The ER doc just used some butterfly bandages and super-glue.

With a fresh application of wax, the Barbour coat looked none the worse for wear. One cannot see the blood stains unless the light hits the coat just right. However the other evening I visited the home of a friend and their pit bull got uncustomarily excited when it came close enough to sniff.

Patricia Lyon-Surrey Fine Art Photography

LETTER 9

Ron,

That really brings it all home to me. The most meaningful theme is the display of dedicated focus. I mean, there you are, a small-town kid in New York City, going for it. Through the pain and all.

I relate. I remember the fitful sleep on the nights before my medical exams.

When there's a lot at stake, my anxiety really heats up, just like yours did before your big audition.

About the car incident: That story shows how you normalize the emotional tension of your performances. "Playing hurt" says it all.

Thanks for the stories.

I'm still fascinated by your ideas about audience and Real Audience. Keep going.

Evelyn

LETTER 10

Evelyn,

It sounds like our emotional experience is quite similar, even though our disciplines and settings are different.

In addressing your observation about the two audiences, I want to clearly state my belief that a masterful performer acknowledges that there are two basic audience sources. They are what I call the Real Audience, which is within the performer, and the Social Audience, which I think of as being the people out there; one interior audience source and one exterior audience source.

I believe that both audience sources are important and that each has a unique contribution to the performance process. The interior Real Audience provides the performer with helpful attitudes and the emotional resources associated with the attitudes. An example would be the emotion of joy associated with the attitude of appreciation. The Social Audience provides social benefits such as the opportunity for social contribution and social connection.

My audience watch in the balcony of the Santa Barbara Symphony concert resulted in the realization that my primary audience source was within me. From that concert on, I weighted it heavily in functional importance, and assigned it the name of Real Audience.

That realization prompted a shift within me. My performance experiences changed for the better: less anxiety and better trumpet playing. No longer was I held captive by an ominous outside force. The Real Audience was within me, and therefore within my field of choice. Theoretically I could choose my own Real Audience. What a curious and liberating thought that was! The next steps suggested themselves. I needed to understand and articulate the nature of a helpful Real Audience and learn how to use it consistently.

Evelyn, I would like to pause in the telling of my story, and ask you the same question that I asked myself at this juncture. How would you describe an audience that is helpful, one that enhances and energizes your performances, one that facilitates full expression of your skill and talent, one that frees you to be yourself, and one that helps you and your performance to be as one?

Ron

LETTER 11

Dear Ron,

That is one interesting question! I know what I don't like. The bottom line is that I really don't like personal rejection, and in some social situations I'm afraid of being put down and embarrassed. I can take on intellectual argument all day long, but personal condemnation of my work, I mean ME, sends me into anxiety central! It hooks my insecurities and it hurts. It also triggers past times when I was helpless and humiliated.

But you are asking about what audience characteristics are helpful. Let's see.

I like it when people trust me, when they cut me some slack, especially after I make an error. I also like when they show appreciation for my efforts, when they specifically name something I've done, and say why they liked it. Yes, I sure do like working for, and with, appreciative people!

Part of that appreciation has to do with the understanding of what I'm doing. You know, the difficulty of the technical challenges. Sometimes I think the only people who get it are my colleagues, the ones who have had to do the same work themselves.

Other than that, I don't know.

Oh, humor. I do better when the tense situations are well lubricated with humor. That's about it. Is that what you were looking for?

Evelyn

LETTER 12

Dear Evelyn,

Thanks for the vulnerability with which you answered my question. I want to clarify what I am looking for by asking you to describe a helpful audience. I'm looking for the attitudes that you associate with such an audience. I'm looking for the attitudes because I believe that the essence of an audience's helpfulness is conveyed and realized within the performer through attitude.

I suspect that when I asked the question, you may have reflected upon an audience that you experienced in a social setting, maybe while you presented a speech, or participated in a student recital, or a school play. You may have been thinking about the people sitting out there in the chairs. Certainly such a reflection helps to answer the question, however I'm considering ALL sources of attitude when I think of audience. I'm thinking that the source of attitude can be found within the performer and also outside the performer. For now, I'd prefer to focus on the attitudes themselves and treat their source(s) as a separate and closely related area of interest.

I heard several distinct helpful attitudes embedded in the narrative of your letter that resonate with my personal and professional experience. I call them attitudes, because they reflect unique dispositional states of mind, as well as internal orientations. When they are present they facilitate performance.

Social Acceptance was the first that you mentioned. The more general attitude is Acceptance itself. You described it in the negative, as fear of social rejection. If we express this in the positive, we get in touch with our need for Social Acceptance – positive connection to something bigger than ourselves. Alfred Adler, an early Viennese psychological theorist, talked about the human need for Belonging. By this he meant social belonging. Again, if we look at the more general and universal human need, it is the attitude of Acceptance itself.

Trust is another attitude that you mentioned. Like you, when I perform facilitated by the presence of Trust, I am emotionally less burdened and not distracted by a need to prove my competence. I am freed to focus on the technical challenges at hand, my performance.

Immediately after Trust, you mentioned being cut some slack. This is important because it addresses the subject of error, and its companion, the spike in emotional tension often present immediately after an error has been made. The attitude that I have found helpful in responding to error is Forgiveness. When I have erred, Self-forgiveness sets me free to generate resilience, which in turn has the effect of minimizing the negative effects of the error. It also acts as an emotional safety net, dissolving and preventing the escalation of excess emotional tension. The overall effect is to allow me to return to an emotional state where I can rise to the level of risk-taking associated with functional, even peak, performance.

You mentioned the helpfulness of appreciative people. Gratitude (Appreciation) is another attitude that facilitates performance. Positive Psychology is a current school of psychology that investigates human strengths rather than pathologies. Associated with this school of thought is Robert Emmons, Ph.D. In his book *Thanks*, he presents current research which validates your observations and personal experience. In a research experiment, a group was encouraged to mindfully journal a listing of their blessings and feelings of gratitude each week over a period of ten weeks. Another contrasting group was encouraged to journal their complaints and burdens. At the end of the ten weeks, surveys were sent to people who knew the participants well. Those associated with the gratitude group rated their group as more helpful than did those associated with the contrasting complaint group.

Another observation of mine, which I believe to be profoundly important, is the relationship between Appreciation (Gratitude) and the emotion of Joy. I have found them to be symbiotic. They travel together, with Appreciation leading the way.

Like you, I experience discomfort when praised. I have learned to transform this discomfort by translating praise statements into Appreciation statements. When people say that I "play great," I translate that to mean that my trumpet playing enhances the quality of their lives and that they appreciate it. After the translation, I find myself appreciating their Appreciation. Isn't it wonderful how that process of amplification works?

After Appreciation you mentioned Understanding. How curious that an Understanding environment would be helpful. You mentioned that your colleagues (I assume medical colleagues) are the only ones that get it.

I call this full-spectrum understanding Empathy. It is full-spectrum because Empathy has intellectual understanding, emotional understanding and understanding of personal intent. Apparently, your medical colleagues have all three. They have had firsthand experience. They have been through a similar refining fire of experience.

Your final comment, describing humor as lubrication, is both metaphorically true and a play on humor itself. Thanks. Whether the humor has its genesis in the comical, the incongruous, or the absurd, it can work wonders in performance. I'll include a story with this letter, *Learnin' to Drive*, which illustrates the power of Playfulness (Playful Humor).

Evelyn, I count six helpful attitudes in your letter: Acceptance, Trust, Forgiveness, Appreciation, Empathy, and Humor (which I call Playfulness). Over the years I have collected only one more. It is Presence. Presence delivers the other six, and is essential in the process we call Performance. You have said that Trust is helpful to you. Would you agree it is helpful only to the degree that it is present?

In closing, please take assurance that the attitudes you listed are the same as those named by others (now in the hundreds) to whom I have asked the same question. There appears to be a universal constellation of attitudes associated with a helpful audience.

I'll await your next letter.

Ron

Learnin' to Drive

She was a petite sixteen-year-old. Pretty dark hair and eyes. French-Canadian descent, but oh my, what a mouth on her, telling me about her learnin' to drive.

"There are two kinds of Shits, the good kind and the bad kind. My uncle's the good kind. My mom's the bad kind. It's so much fuckin' fun when my uncle's teachin' me to drive his big truck. He takes me out to his cornfield. We drive around the outside. If I hit a cornstalk, he says, "You've just killed another one." Or, "You just taken the arm off that one." "Oh look, you've just decapitated him." We just laugh and have a good ol' time. I'm pretty good with that truck. It has that fuckin' clutch on the floor. It doesn't even shake anymore when I take off. I don't hit the corn anymore either.

My mom doesn't understand why I can drive a big fuckin' shift truck and can't drive her automatic Subaru Outback. She screams every fuckin' time I just get a little out of the center of the lane. I get so fuckin' uptight with her! I hate drivin' with her. I'm no good at drivin' that car. She's so fuckin' stupid. She doesn't GET IT. She's the bad kind of Shit."

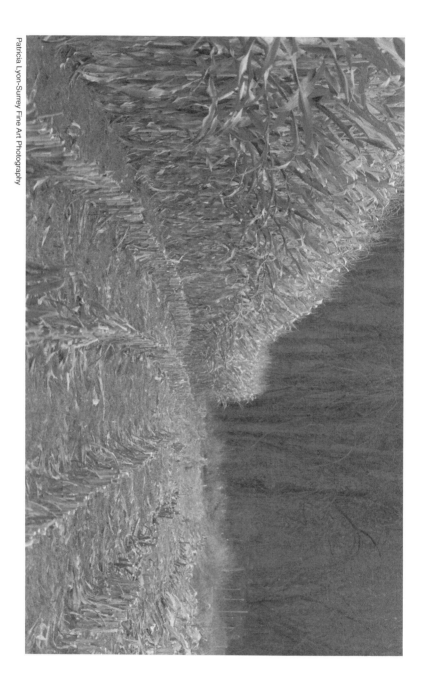

LETTER 13

Dear Ron,

What a hoot! Makes me want to go out driving with her uncle. I've always thought of attitude as important, but not to the degree that you stress. I've always concentrated on how things were going, so this is a new emphasis. Not that anything you are saying is particularly strange or unfamiliar. I've grown up with statements like: "Your attitude determines your altitude." Or: "Just do your best. That's all you can do." All these cultural statements are part of the fabric of my life. Each one certainly carries attitude. So you are saying that the attitudinal nature of these self-statements is critical to my performance outcomes, and perhaps, my performance anxiety. Let's not forget that. I know that my anxiety has a lot to do with outcomes.

Am I getting your message? Are attitudes a big deal, perhaps the biggest deal?

Evelyn

LETTER 14

Dear Evelyn,

In a word... Yes. The attitudinal nature of your performance process is a big deal. For now, let's not be focused on which part of the performance process is the most important. My interest is to offer you my understanding of the whole. One of my observations is that the creative performance process needs encouraging attitude to exist. Another is that the nature of the attitudinal content is a primary determiner of performance anxiety and performance outcome.

Masterful Life-Performance says that there exists a constellation of attitudes, when present within the performer, that is helpful in inviting more functional performance. It also says that these attitudes are necessary to achieve the degree of risk necessary for peak performance. Seven of these attitudes are Acceptance, Forgiveness, Trust, Empathy, Playfulness, Presence, and Appreciation.

The exciting thing for me was the realization that these were within my own field of choice (in my own head). But before I fully engaged with the concept and practice of exercising this sense of choice, my interest led me in another direction. I found myself wanting to examine attitude a bit more.

Evelyn, you know that I spent about a decade of my life studying and practicing electrical engineering. During that time I was introduced to many theoretical concepts. One of these came from Calculus. It had to do with asking the question: What is the form of a mathematical function, as a part of that function (a variable) takes on values approaching infinity? Applying this thinking to the helpful attitudes associated with creative performance, I asked myself the question: What describes the form of the most helpful audience, the infinitely most helpful audience, the Ideal Audience? I puzzled over this for several months, and finally arrived at a solution which satisfied me. I arrived at the word "unconditional."

To me, the infinitely most helpful audience was one that could be described as Unconditionally Accepting, Unconditionally Forgiving, Unconditionally Trusting, Unconditionally Empathic,

Unconditionally Playful, Unconditionally Present, and Unconditionally Appreciative.

I was fascinated by this realization, but curiously, not surprised. The few attitudes that I had identified, and the idea that their pure unconditional form would be the most helpful, were intuitively self-evident. I was talking to myself about the unconditional nature and power of love; love as actualized and expressed through attitude. I was proving to myself, through a rather circuitous path, that love was (and is) an essential facet of my own creative performance process.

I also realized that I had embraced another dimension of my own creative process. The constellation of unconditionally loving attitudes was more than descriptive. It was, and *IS*, my Ideal Audience.

Evelyn, I need some reassurance here. Does this make sense to you so far? Is my theoretical path helpful to you?

Ron

LETTER 15

Dear Ron,

Your idea that the constellation of loving attitudes is your Ideal Audience challenges my imagination. It's two steps removed from where I was when I first wrote you asking for your ideas on managing anxiety. Back then I thought the only audience was the people out there. Now you're taking me on a wild ride into a world of abstractions. I'm worried that I will never be able to use ML-P because I might not ever really understand it.

I get the importance of helpful attitudes. I get that the audience inside me is the most influential (Real) one. I get that I can choose the attitudes I bring to my performances.

But this business about the "Real Audience" *being* the attitudes is a bit too big a step. Help! Tell me how I can access this abstract audience. I'd like to be able to use it.

Tell me how you use it, and then I'll decide if I can give it a try.

Evelyn

LETTER 16

Dear Evelyn,

Your confusion is understandable. I've been working with these concepts in all manner of creative endeavors for many years. Even with this history, I find that I need self-awareness and self-prompting to stay with the process.

The first thing that I do is to acknowledge that the presence of the Ideal Audience is accessed and accessible through invitation. I believe it is a gift from the Universe, and is to be invited, not controlled. In this respect, Masterful Performance is an act of profound humility.

To answer your question more directly: I focus my consciousness on what I call an Ideal Audience Cue. This is a mind's eye visual and/or verbal Cue, which I deliberately choose because it prompts in me one or more of the Ideal Audience attitudes. The Cue is meaningful to me because I have searched for it, and found it embedded in my own life experience. Again, let me use your life experience to illustrate.

Please answer the following question: When I say the words "unconditional acceptance, unconditional forgiveness, unconditional trust, unconditional empathy, unconditional playfulness, unconditional presence, and unconditional appreciation," what person, place, or thing immediately comes to mind?

Ron

LETTER 17

Dear Ron,

There are several things that rush into my mind. You may laugh, but the first one is my dog, Champ, my seven-year-old Irish Setter. I can just see his bright adoring eyes, his wide-open panting mouth, and his big slobbery tongue. For seven years he has been an unfailing source of unconditional love for me.

Next, my grandfather comes to mind. His weathered face always lit up when he saw me coming. He was exceedingly smart, and totally opinionated, but he loved my opinions and favored acceptance of me over arguing me down. He trusted me far more than I trusted myself.

My mother comes to mind. She was just as opinionated as her father, but far more direct with me. When she offered her opinion, which she often did, she always qualified it as her opinion, and acknowledged that it might be different from mine. I don't know how many times she said, "Here's what I'm thinking... but I believe you know more than you think you know." I always felt a genuine caring and trust behind her interactions with me. She wanted me to thrive and be self-assured. "Just do your best, Honey, and let the cards fall where they may."

I have one more: God. When you said Unconditional Presence, I immediately flashed on God. My vision of God is that of an unconditional love source.

Ron, is this what you meant?

Evelyn

LETTER 18

Dear Evelyn,

That is exactly what I had in mind when I posed the question to you. I call the four you mentioned (Champ, grandfather's face, mother's presence and words, and your vision of God) your Ideal Audience Cues. When you choose to bring any of the four into your consciousness, you invite into your being the attitude(s) you associate with the Cue. In that sense, your being becomes infused with the attitude. And along with the attitude comes the emotion associated with the attitude. One of the clearest examples of this is the coupling between the attitude of Appreciation and the emotion of Gladness (Joy).

I am enclosing four more stories. Each of these stories (*Dog Story, Grampa Red, Mom, Speaking in Tongues*) illustrate another person's use of a specific Cue that you mentioned. My intent is to demonstrate the universality of this process. I believe we all use it, knowingly or not.

Ron

Dog Story

A man in his early thirties, a bit disheveled, came off the street rather unexpectedly into the waiting room of my office. Said he needed to talk to someone. I didn't have a client that hour, so I asked him into my office.

He looked the dark soul, a very depressed presence. Said he was in despair. He was losing his job, had little money, his wife wanted a divorce, and he was thinking about killing himself.

After the standard depression/suicide, drug/alcohol screening questions, I concluded that he was not in imminent danger of suicide, although the possibility was there. His behaviors indicated that he was desperately looking for a way to restore his life. I figured I had one crack at helping him.

We roughed out his life story, and I spent the remainder of the time helping him define his helpful audience attitudes, beginning to develop in him a Masterful Life-Performance consciousness.

"Have you experienced these attitudes from any source? From any person, place or thing?" I asked.

Emphatically and sadly he replied, "No. That's a black hole. You see, my parents ritually abused me for the first seventeen years of my life until I left my home."

Then he remarked thoughtfully, "Oh, my dog... My dog was like that toward me."

"Is your dog still alive?"

"No," he said.

"It makes no difference – attitudes have a life beyond death. Do you have a picture of your dog?"

"No, but my mother in California has a snapshot."

"Get the photo and carry a copy of it in your wallet. Each time you feel confused, sad, anxious, or angry, reflect on the presence of your dog then apply the loving attitude to whatever is troubling you."

He said he would get back to me. I gave him my card.

Two weeks later he made an appointment and showed up on time.

He looked brighter, was reasonably well groomed and seemed eager to talk.

"My wife doesn't know what's come over me. She's stopped wanting a divorce. And I'm doing okay at work. I don't understand what has happened."

"I believe you have experienced, perhaps for the first time in your life, that you have the choice of performing your life to your own helpful interior audience, as cued up by the photo presence of your beloved dog. This insight has led to an inner process that has transformed your inner response to outer emotional and social challenges."

This inner change had a profoundly positive effect on others in his social world and dissolved much of his inner angst and tension. In short, he had experienced a spiritual attitudinal transformation.

He thanked me and left. I didn't see him again. I don't know if the process stuck. But I do know that for at least a brief time in his difficult life, he intentionally invited and was subsequently gifted with a loving attitude toward self.

Grampa Red

My friend and colleague, Gail, is supremely competent in her social, analytical, organizational and musical skills. She's a big-hearted visionary soprano of a person; direct and intelligently expressive. The vein of insecurity running through her early adult life always baffled me, until she began talking about how her mother's hyper-scrutinizing style defined a narrow social role for Gail within the family. This limiting definition of what it meant to behave as a female was reinforced by the cultural norms of mid-twentieth century American gender inequality. However, genetics were definitely in her favor, as she inherited the talents of her successful, extroverted, scientist-salesman father. Now in her early fifties, a confident professional, she has accomplished a strong sense of gender equality. It is clear to me that she has done the social-psychological work of several generations.

One of her milestone breakthroughs in musical performance involved a brush with Masterful Life-Performance. She had just accepted the lead role of Anna in a Canadian community theater production of *The King and I.*

As she related her performance story to me, she said that her first "Oh Shit Moment" was when the script and music were delivered to her, and she saw the magnitude of the project. She had not done any musical theater in fifteen years, and never anything of this complexity. Shortly after this moment of frightening realization she called for a consult. We met over lunch.

Before finishing our meal, I was confident that she could, and would, arrive at technical mastery of the material. Knowing Gail, talent was not the problem. The problem was that her approach to performance was a fear-based one, and invited excess emotional tension (performance anxiety, stage fright). She was in the process of trying to get personal validation from her projected Canadian troupe and her projected Canadian audience. Gail believed that the only Real Audience was the group of people who would buy their tickets and attend the performances. I introduced her to a radically different understanding of performance. I asked her to consider that the only social goal of her performance be to gift the people in the seats her Anna. I asked her to consider a radical change to her vision of audience as well.

We talked about the Real Audience being within her. We talked about what audience attitudes are helpful to the performer. We talked about how to build and access one's helpful Internal Audience through choosing to use one's unique helpful Internal Audience Cues, a Cue being a person, place or thing strongly associated with actual loving life experience.

When I listed my collection of helpful attitudes (unconditional acceptance, forgiveness, trust, empathy, playfulness, presence and appreciation), and asked her to notice what person, place, or thing came to her mind, a sweet knowing smile flowed across her face. She wistfully told me about her childhood experience with "Grampa Red." She mentioned a locket her mother had given her containing a picture of Red as a young soldier.

Her step-grandfather, Red, had come into the life of Gail's grief-stricken grandmother after Gail's grandfather died in a bomber crash over Nuremberg. Granny's extreme grief and accompanying depression began to lift only after Grampa Red began seeing her regularly. Eventually he wooed her into marriage.

Red himself had survived the war, having served on several battlefields as an artillerist, whose primary duty was to maintain and repair artillery. Years of war had taken its toll. His lungs, hearing, and emotional functioning were all damaged. Eventually he died an early death at 59, but not too soon to leave young Gail infused with his loving attention and unconditional adoration. Gail's audience Cue was planted deep in her life experience.

The King and I turned out to be one of the highlights of her musical performance life. There were thirteen performances to packed houses. Even though she was plagued with illness and extreme vocal fatigue, she experienced a consistent sense of stage calmness. The calmness came as a welcome surprise and a profound pleasure.

During all performances, Gail wore a small gold chain and locket around her neck. Inside the locket was a tiny photo of a man in a World War II Army uniform.

Mom

Two days' worth of dirty dishes are in my kitchen sink. Sitting at the bare kitchen table I slip the thermometer out from under my sore tongue. Just about 102 degrees. I haven't felt this weak in a long time. Must be some kind of flu, or mono or something.

I'm not going to miss the concert tonight. Not for anything. I'm totally lucky to be performing, accepted into the trumpet section of the National Orchestral Association Orchestra, New York City's most prestigious youth orchestra. It's my first year at Juilliard. It's my first concert with the NOA and it's in Carnegie Hall. I'm not going to miss this one. No, not for anything.

• • •

The stage lights out here are really bright, and way too hot. I'm way too hot. My tux is already sweated out. From my chair in the back of the orchestra I look out into the great hall. All I see is balcony on top of balcony. There must be five or six levels. Like giant rows of teeth, just waiting to devour. The sweat is running off my forehead. It's in my eyes. God, I hope I will be able to see the baton.

There's the downbeat. Off we go. And in a flash, all that remains is the trumpet part before me, the magnificent tonal colors and pulse of the orchestra, the baton and my mom's California sun-drenched face. Just like when she would sunbathe in our back yard, listening to the Yankee-Dodger games on the radio. I play to her. Her loving spirit infuses me with calm.

I play full-toned and with precision. My white-hot focus lasts throughout the whole concert. How can this be? How do I play this well in such a weakened condition?

Speaking In Tongues

"My life is falling apart," she said. Her seventeen-year marriage was crumbling. Her emotionally and physically distant husband had at long last embraced his true sexuality, and was dating a man. Divorce was imminent. With five kids, money would be scarce. Years before, cerebral palsy had left the right side of her body noticeably compromised, and her nonfunctional right hand was smaller than her left. A short list of resources included: great kids, a high likelihood of keeping the small but adequate house, a strong God-centered faith and a love and talent for stage acting. She wanted to talk with me because an important audition was coming up. In spite of her love of acting, she was going to forgo the audition. Her performance anxiety was too formidable.

She saw herself as a frightened actor wanting to perform, rather than my view of a frightened performer wanting to act. She believed that acting had been one of the very few venues where she had gotten approval and positive social attention. In her present state of vulnerability, she was not going to risk disappointment due to a failed audition. In fact, she had passed over many auditions in the emotionally demanding preceeding years. And yet, it was clear that she wanted a part in that play. She wanted it very much. She wanted it at that specific time in her life, and she wanted me to show her how to get it.

Fortunately her personal resources were abundant. Besides having the commanding voice, countenance, and stage presence of a natural thespian, her personal spirituality had been the centerpiece of her life for decades. We talked about the nature of Masterful Performance, and how she could invite her whole self into her stage performance without needing to control the outcome. We talked about how to develop and access her helpful internal audience.

She won her audition. She did it by performing for the producer and to her unconditional interior audience (her vision of an unconditionally loving and accepting God). Since that pivotal time in her life, she has acted successfully in several plays and many other performances. The other day I asked her how her acting was going. She said, "Quite well. I enjoy sharing my talent with the actors and people in the audience, rather than competing with the other actors, as I used to do. I enjoy showing people me, and not just the cerebral palsy."

"What about your internal audience?"

"Before I go out, I find a quiet place, and I speak in tongues."

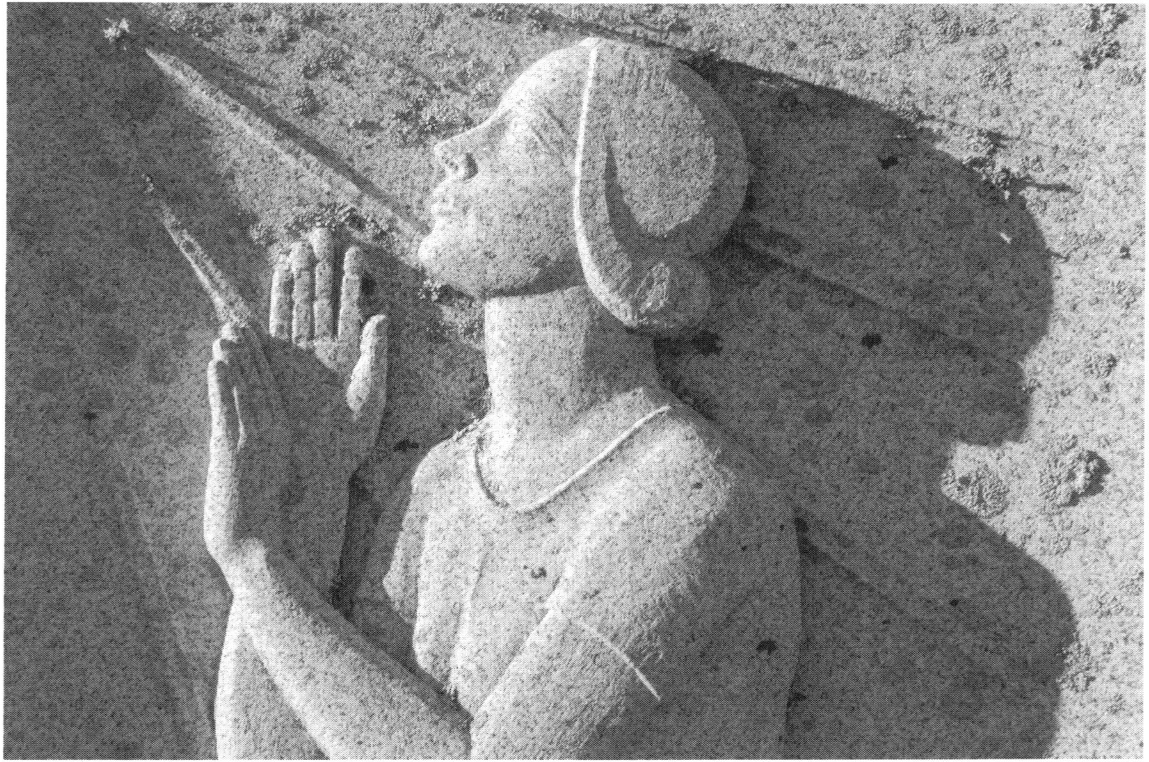

Patricia Lyon-Surrey Fine Art Photography

LETTER 19

Dear Ron,

I'm beginning to understand how you, and others, use internal cues to deal with anxiety and to get through peak stress times. However my life is plagued with an element of persistent tension. It's the irritating emotional background noise that I deal with day after day. The stress is there just about all the time, and the occasional performance can introduce a tsunami that can swamp me. I find it hard to believe that this Masterful Life-Performance process could erase my constant tension. How do you deal with constant stress? I know that your life isn't a bowl of cherries. You must deal with lots of stress, performing the variety of life roles you have chosen and that have chosen you. You have a fully invested life, just like I have. How do you manage your excess day-to-day anxiety?

Evelyn

LETTER 20

Dear Evelyn,

Your letter brought a smile to my face, because of your insight and the commonality of our human condition. At least you are not asking *why* questions. *Why* questions would introduce another order of complexity. I like *how* questions. Engineers ask *how* questions. *How* questions invite movement forward. They invite solutions.

Your specific question, about how to address ambient emotional stress, is an important one. It is important because sustained excess emotional stress damages bodies (brains) and all manner of human health. The destructive compensation behaviors (for instance all of the negative addictions) are everyday examples of behaviors driven by excess emotional stress states. I believe that the solutions to excess emotional tension in critical situations, such as important public performances, shed light on the ambient stress challenges. We can learn to live in such a way so as to regulate excess ambient stress through lessons learned in high stress circumstances. Stress is not the enemy. Emotional tension is the angel of liveliness and the purveyor of meaningfulness. The creative Flow State of peak performance is associated with emotional tension. It is the *excess* tension that needs trimming.

I've included a figure showing the relationship between performance and emotional tension. It looks like a mountain, with the mountain peak corresponding to peak performance. Note that one does not move toward the peak without an accompanying increase in emotional tension. This is the helpful tension. However, there is a point at which increased tension detracts from performance. And there is an exit point at which the Zone, or Flow State, associated with peak performance is breached. Emotional tension beyond this point is destructive. In public performance, this excess is often described as nervousness or stage fright. In day-to-day living, excess anxiety can be experienced as unsettled feelings and a state of general discontent.

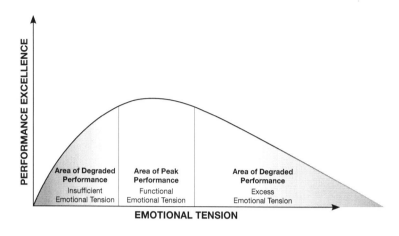

Figure 1

I use the same process of emotional regulation for day-to-day living that I use for stage performance. If it works in high anxiety settings, why would it not work in low-to-medium anxiety settings? And why would I exclude its use from the performance of day-to-day living? For me it is not distracting, and it is comforting. It helps me in my quest to be a high-functioning human being. I like processes that work. When the ambient excess anxiety is relentless, I believe that the regulation process needs to be relentless as well. If my interior repetitive thought process takes on the flavor of compulsivity, so what! I'm the performer. I'm the one who is out there taking on the risks of my everyday living. I'm the one taking the heat. In the role of performer, I can choose any strategy that leads to meeting my needs and the needs of those around me.

A significant source of direction and inspiration comes from stories of my heroes, people who have demonstrated how to live in powerful, life-affirming ways. Two of them are Louis Armstrong, a celebrated jazz musician, and Viktor Frankl, a philosopher-psychologist and Holocaust survivor. One story that I have included here is an example of ML-P used in a specific high-tension music performance. The other shows its use in the extremely inhumane and life-threatening environment of a Nazi death camp.

Ron

Satchmo

As a young trumpet player I derived great delight from listening to and performing the music of my New Orleans Dixieland trumpet hero, Louis Armstrong. One of the first books I read was *Satchmo*, an autobiography. As an adult I happened on a used book, *Trumpeter's Tale, the Story of Young Louis Armstrong*, by Jeanette Eaton. There I found another compelling example of the Masterful Life-Performance consciousness in the following story.

In 1932 Louis's manager arranged for a tour of Britain, including a final appearance at the Music Hall in London. Since this was at the very beginning of Louis's rise to fame his first reaction was one of trepidation. But he did indeed play at the Music Hall, and during that performance a loud request for *Tiger Rag* came from many in the audience. Louis had not programmed this piece because he thought it was too dated to be known in England. He was delighted with the request.

As his band began the old tune and he immersed himself in the music, he reported being transported back to the performance world of his New Orleans youth. There were no evening clothes, no concert hall, no vast British audience, only he and his barefoot friends singing their hearts out to the folks of Perdido Street. In his mind's eye he could see all the colorful characters there. When *Tiger Rag* finished and the trumpet came off his lips, the fantasy was replaced by waves of thunderous applause and cheers.

Louis Armstrong's Cues to unconditional acceptance and unconditional appreciation were the music itself, and his visual memories of the pimps, whores, and customers of Storyville, the New Orleans Red Light District. They were the ones who threw coins out their windows and cheered for the little quartet of boys singing for them from the sidewalk.

Twenty years later, these unconditional attitudes were released again within Louis. The London morning journals described the audience reaction as "a mass demonstration of incredible proportions." [187]

Satchmo, Jack Bradley publicity photograph of Louis Armstrong in 1961.
Courtesy of the Louis Armstrong House Museum

The Bird

"Then I grasped the greatest secret that human poetry and human thought
and belief have to impart: the salvation of man is through love and in love."[49]
—Viktor Frankl

I would like to refer you to a story, rare in its poignancy. It can
be found in Viktor Frankl's *Man's Search For Meaning*, the autobio-
graphical account of his experiences in Nazi forced-labor and death
camps. Although his book is replete with examples of spiritual and
psychological insights gained amidst unspeakable human conditions,
for me this story stands out as an excellent example of the mastery
of life performance and the importance of the role and nature of the
Internal Audience.

The setting is an early frigid morning at a camp worksite, his
detachment of exhausted and starved Jewish slaves wielding pickaxes
in the ground of a frozen ditch. Earlier their Nazi guards had severely
beaten those who had stumbled and fallen along the rocky way to the
site. Viktor Frankl's wife figures prominently in this excerpt.

> *"For hours I stood hacking at the icy ground. The guard*
> *passed by, insulting me, and once again I communed with my*
> *beloved. More and more I felt that she was present, that she*
> *was with me; I had the feeling that I was able to touch her,*
> *able to stretch out my hand and grasp hers. The feeling was*
> *very strong: she was there. Then, at that very moment, a bird*
> *flew down silently and perched just in front of me, on a heap*
> *of soil that I had dug up from the ditch, and looked steadily*
> *at me."* [52]

Patricia Lyon-Surrey Fine Art Photography

LETTER 21

Dear Ron,

Reading your stories moved me. Very tender stories. Thank you.
I see how cues can be used for mood regulation and performance in
everyday (even life-threatening) circumstances. It seems you're saying
that both stories are basically the same, and differ only in intensity
and duration. You are advocating the carrying of one's personal Ideal
Audience Cue continually, for use anytime that life becomes demanding. This is your way of regulating your emotions and remaining
highly functional in difficult situations.

It sounds like something I could try when my anxiety starts to
get uncomfortably high. I don't think it's an easy fix. I think it is a
discipline, a practiced discipline. I think you really have to be sold on
the truth of the process to use it habitually.

I like the idea that I don't have to erase all of my anxiety, and need
only to address the excess. That's a bit more manageable. Erasing all
the anxiety is way too much work, and seems like an exaggerated, even
false, way to approach life. I don't mind tension, even if it's a bit of a
pain. I just don't like it when it gets in the way of doing something I
want to do. I mean performing in a way that I like to perform. Or, for
that matter, when it gets just too damned uncomfortable.

Another thing I like is the insight that this process is love-based.
Viktor Frankl's experience brought that point home. For that matter,
so did Louis Armstrong's concert. They were just very different settings.
Thanks for showing me a glimpse of the universality.

Each of the attitudes that you associate with the Ideal Audience is a
loving attitude. You are saying that the way to invite creative performance
is through love. But I want to improve. I want to get better, and I think I
have to be critical of my performance to get there. I have always believed
that the only way for me to keep improving is to demand it of myself, demanding perfection. You keep talking about inviting peak performance.
That doesn't sound like demand language. Tell me more about the
love-based nature of Masterful Life-Performance.

Evelyn

LETTER 22

Dear Evelyn,

You are addressing one of the critical points of Masterful Life-Performance: How to get better. How to improve your game, your performance, your technical expertise, in whatever setting that might be.

In my youth, my trumpet teachers, my school teachers, my sports coaches, my Irish intergenerational family values, my Christianity, and my North American masculine cultural values all taught me that Perfectionism was The Way. Perfectionistic goals and values were necessary and preferred. There was only one way to improve. Strive for perfection. Put forth a 100% effort, maybe even 110%. If the performance is not absolutely perfect, don't be satisfied. Never be content. If I am satisfied with less than perfection, I'll never attain it. I'll never get better. Keep demanding perfection. Work harder, practice longer, keep my nose to the grindstone. During several adolescent summers I averaged seven hours of trumpet practice daily.

As Masterful Life-Performance evolved, I began to understand that Perfectionism could carry a performer (me) just so far. I began to see Perfectionism as a form of self-limitation, even self-abuse, and that it relied on the notion that one could (and *should*) beat oneself up into perfection. It assumed that perfection was attainable, sustainable and desirable. I began to understand that chronically beating oneself up (especially emotionally) had only one predictable result: being beaten up! I learned that Perfectionism can lead to the loss of emotional health, a loss of the sense of calm gladness. In my psychological studies I learned that Perfectionism is associated with anxiety and depressive disorders.

My yellow brick road of early successes had reinforced my belief in Perfectionism. Evelyn, please note that the first audition I'd ever lost was for a chair in the Philadelphia Orchestra... at age 21. It was a shock. I had a long painful walk ahead of me, to find my way out of my Perfectionist life box.

Within my dominant culture there was no clearly defined, emotionally healthy substitute paradigm for Perfectionism. There was no paradigm available to me by which to honor my fascination with, and my pursuit of, excellence. So I invented one: Excellism. I began to think of myself as an Excellist, a performer who loves the pursuit of excellence. Always my Perfectionism had been associated with fear: fear of making a mistake, fear of not achieving my goals, fear of losing my reputation, or my skills, or this or that. You get the picture. I noticed that, as I began the development of an interior loving "Audience," an exciting increase in artistic expression began to appear. It was particularly apparent to me in my trumpet performance. It was the more-relaxed excellence that I had been wanting all along. Being hard on myself decreased as the attitudes of self-forgiveness and self-acceptance grew. My anxiety and sadness were diminished as well. Masterful Life-Performance, and its complementary correlate, Excellism, became my personal territory ahead.

As I began sharing my ideas, I gained the understanding that I was not alone in this journey. I have included a story of one such fellow Perfectionist who benefitted as he embraced the love-based Excellist philosophy of performance.

Ron

Ferrari Mind

The man sitting across from me in my office, telling me his story, prompted flashbacks of my days as a student in the electrical engineering department at the University of California at Santa Barbara. This guy's mind worked fast, like the geniuses in my classes who read engineering texts like they were romance novels. A Ferrari mind. His story was a sad one, full of loss. Somewhere along the way, after graduation from Cal Tech, he had shared his computer software idea with a trusted colleague, only to find out that the colleague went on to claim authorship of the idea. The idea's ultimate commercial value was well over 100 million dollars, of which none came his way.

But this man had not sought me out to talk about this disappointment. Even though he was a successful businessman and a master yoga instructor, his passion had taken a different path.

Put simply, his ambition was to write a historical novel, but he couldn't. In fact he could not write the novel's first full paragraph. And this was true in spite of having done extensive historical research and having been told by lettered people that he was a talented writer. He had even traveled to his favorite quaint Dutch hotel in Amsterdam for inspiration to get over his writer's block. The file in his computer entitled "Novel" came back to America empty. He smiled when I told him my fee. He said, "That's what I pay for one night at a hotel. If your stuff works even a little, it's well worth it to me."

The next two hours went by quickly. As I gathered his life story, especially the information leading to his extreme perfectionistic attitudes towards his writing, it became clear that he needed a blueprint to unconditionality. He had developed some of the critical parts of the ML-P process. The helpful visual Cue for unconditionality came from his relationships with his yoga colleagues, with whom he had experienced extensive unconditional, life-affirming attitudes. Among the concepts that I suggested to him was that he fire his unhelpful Interior Audience Cue, and replace it with his yoga colleague Cue.

His unhelpful audience Cue had been learned through early familial experiences and carried, unchallenged, into his adult years.

I told him that a helpful first step in the creative process is to realize that we have the freedom (and the wisdom) to choose our Internal Audience Cue. It can be the first choice that we, as creative performers, make. The second choice is to choose a Cue that is helpful, one that prompts felt sources of previous and specific life-affirming attitudinal experience.

I said, "The discipline is to keep the helpful Cue in our conscious-ness, especially as we encounter specific difficulties and emotional challenges."

He said, "From my yoga practice I'm familiar with discipline."

He lapped up the Masterful Life-Performance consciousness like a thirsty animal. He left full of enthusiasm, and with the unprompted promise that he would process the ideas for a couple weeks and get back to me. Several weeks passed and he didn't get back to me. I called him. A cheerful voice said, "During the second day after our visit, I sat down with my word processor and wrote my novel's first full paragraph... I couldn't write, and now I can."

It's been six months since that first phone inquiry. Last week I heard from a mutual friend that he's still writing.

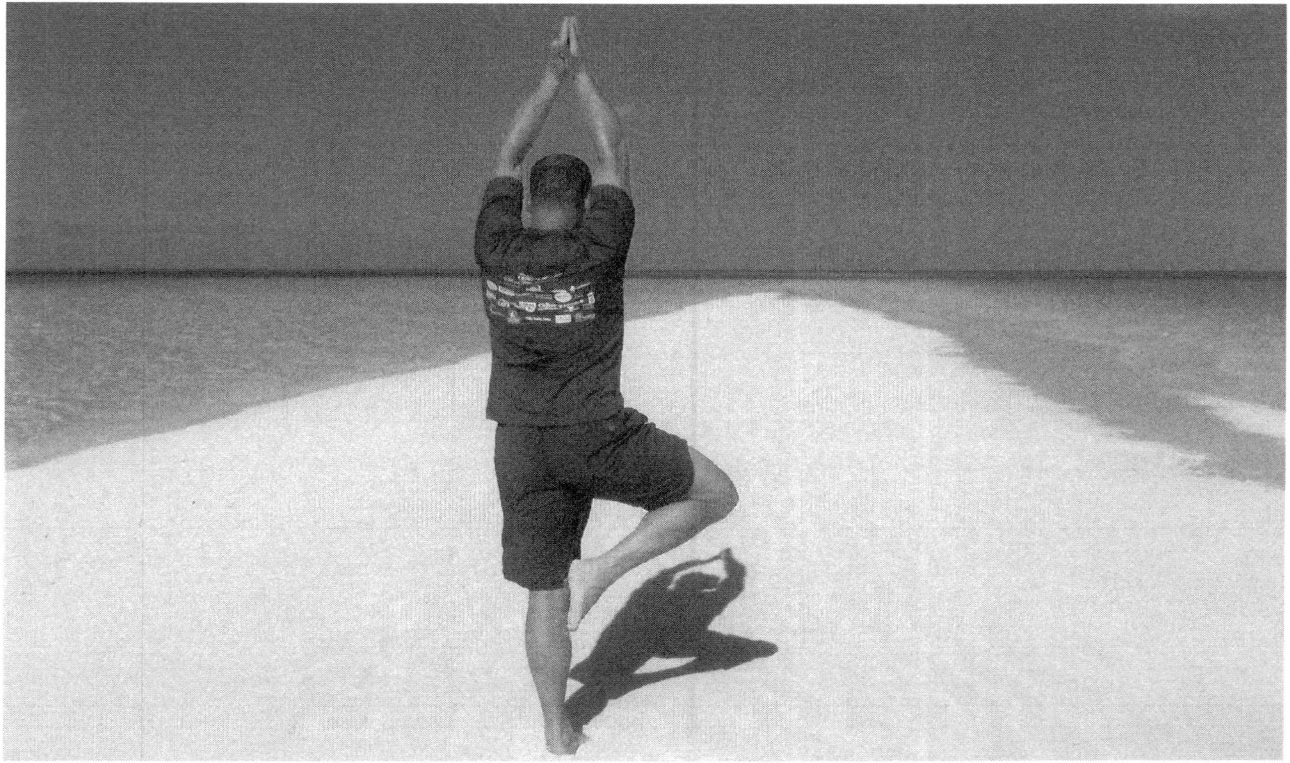
Patricia Lyon-Surrey Fine Art Photography

LETTER 23

Dear Ron,

Ferrari Mind broadsided me. I wonder how many things I've thought about doing, and had the resources to do, and didn't even start. I always say, "I'll do it in my next life," and laugh it off. But what I'm really saying is that I'd like to do it now, and what I do now probably won't meet my expectations.

I think you're right. Perfectionism gets in the way. I don't really fear failure. What I fear is the self-condemnation I inflict on myself when things don't go according to my sometimes-inflated expectations. And then I have to face feeling a painful sadness. I remember you saying sadness is associated with loss. In my case I guess what I lose is my positive sense of self, my self-esteem. That really hurts. No wonder I don't make my move to get started.

Your *Ferrari Mind* guy and I have a lot in common. Unconditional love, in his case as applied to self, worked well. I wonder what would happen if I chose to use it too. That's a moot question. On some level I'm already trying it out.

Also I think you are right on about Perfectionism being a personal philosophy that is toxic to all that we do. It has carried me far (career-wise all the way to a successful medical practice). But at what cost? A big part of me feels beaten up. I'm really tired of being anxious about everything. What I want is a break from the self-inflicted, self-limiting, self-exhausting Perfectionism. And I want to use my emotional resources on what I care about, my performance within my various life roles. I want to live with a sense of emotional focus, not wasting my emotional energy on worry. I want this to be a part of my daily life, my lifestyle.

I like your idea about Excellism. Cool concept, Ron! It leaves me with optimism about seeking improvement and fulfillment. I, like you, love when I do an excellent job, or when I see someone else do an excellent job. It's exciting and life-affirming to me.

Still, I remain a bit confused and anxious about making mistakes.

I'm uncomfortable with the inevitable error associated with my work, my projects, my performances. What about error?

Evelyn

Evelyn,

Error is a fascinating subject. Performing from the viewpoint of Perfectionism, we choose as our primary performance goal the elimination of all error, all mistakes. We avoid worthwhile and productive pursuits, distracted by the overwhelming goal of avoiding error. We avoid potentially productive risk-laden projects. When we under-risk life, it loses excitement and meaning. Perfectionism leaves our lives compromised. But you asked about error.

I can say with assurance that it is always present. It is just a matter of how it is defined. Design engineers always take error into account, because they plan for real world functionality. They use the concept of tolerances. All functional systems are designed with tolerances which define the range of error. If the tolerances are too small or too large, the functionality of the design is compromised. Engineers want their designs to work. We want our performances to work.

The only place where zero tolerance exists is in the imagination of the Perfectionist. I think of Perfectionists as living in LaLa Land. Evelyn, this is my tongue-in-cheek term for an unreal and destructive consciousness. The demand of the Perfectionist is that the real world, which is alive with error, be errorless. When the impossible is demanded, the result is generally less than what could have been realized with the acceptance of ever-present error.

One common subtle form of Perfectionist demand is the use, or implied use, of the word *should*.

Earlier I mentioned the concept-word *should*. *Should* thinking is perfectionistic because it demands a reality that isn't. He should have lost some weight (but he didn't). She should be a better mother (but she isn't). I should not have made that mistake in my performance (but I did). If applied to the future, it produces pushback tension. One of the most effective ways to keep a person in a present pattern of behavior is to say that they should change. When is the last time a person stopped smoking because they thought they should? The pushback comes from our freedom of choice being compromised. We are creative choice makers, and react with emotional tension when our choice making is challenged. Alfred Adler, the early psychological theorist, was quick to advise his patients to stop *shoulding* on themselves.

When the Perfectionist encounters unacceptable error (any error at all) in performance, the error can prompt an irritating emotional distraction, which can result in a loss of focus and increased error. Excellism, the love-based approach to performance, minimizes error-prompted irritation.

Excellists plan for the possibility, even probability, of error. They are operating in the real world. Because of their love-based attitudes (one of which is acceptance), they are able to accept more of what the given circumstance presents, including the presence of error. They recognize that the real world is alive with error, and planning for the possibility of error is a way of inviting a reduction in anxiety. A well-planned performance includes an error risk assessment, and the accompanying expectations. It is not a matter of what should be. It is a matter of what could be, given a thorough acceptance of what is known about the conditions of the performance. Excellists always have expectations, but their range of expectation is significantly wider than that of Perfectionists. They are surprised a whole lot less often.

In my mind, Vladimir Horowitz, the legendary virtuoso pianist, was an Excellist. He gave the following description of his performance process: "I must tell you I take terrible risks. Because my playing is very clear, when I make a mistake, you hear it. If you want me to play only the notes without any specific dynamics, I will never make one mistake. Never be afraid to dare." Another quote attributed to him is my favorite: When asked why he makes so many mistakes, he responded: "Do you want to hear perfection, or do you want to hear Horowitz?"

Evelyn, does this put error and mistakes in a somewhat different light?

Ron

LETTER 25

Ron,

I like several things you said: Error is always present in the real world; there is a real cost when the only goal is to totally eliminate error; and anxiety is magnified when I "should on myself." I also like the idea of risk assessment, directly facing the best guess range of how things may actually go.

I can see where the Excellist approach could take a lot of the sting of fear away, especially when I focus on delivering the performance without the distraction of worrying so much about making a mistake.

It's not easy for me to imagine myself as enlightened as Horowitz, but he gives me a clearer goal. He certainly approaches his performances with a set of attitudes different from mine.

Could you give me more about each of the attitudes you have chosen? Remember, I'm coming with a history of Perfectionism. I need lots of explanation… and time. I have spent decades with my perfectionistic habits. I need time to ponder.

Evelyn

LETTER 26

Evelyn,

It is an important, and always reassuring, exercise for me to review the seven attitudes of the Ideal Interior Audience that I have found to be of critical importance to my own life performance. Thanks for asking. I'll start with Unconditional Acceptance.

To me, the attitude of Unconditional Acceptance is the capacity to receive without reservation. The totality of the performance is acknowledged, recognized, and received without judgment or evaluation. There exists an openness to what is. An uncensored, unfiltered willingness to receive that which is offered. The performance reality is welcomed in its entirety… no strings attached… no obstructions… no fear. All the accuracies and inaccuracies, the helpful and unhelpful parts, the beautiful and the ugly, and the functional and dysfunctional are embraced without conditions attached.

The attitude of Unconditional Acceptance invites Flow, the state in which the performer and the performance are as one. An absorbing, calm curiosity is present. The performer is set free to exercise sufficient risk to actualize and maximize the excellence of the performance. I believe that the highly creative state of Flow is possible only with the presence of Unconditional Acceptance. It is a necessary attitude for the gift of Flow to make its appearance.

Children can display levels of Unconditional Acceptance, especially Unconditional Self-Acceptance, that are truly impressive. I've included a story of an eight-year-old beginning trumpet student of mine, which illustrates his attitude of Unconditional Self-Acceptance.

I have included a second story, which illustrates how a person's creative process can be facilitated by learning how to access and use Unconditional Acceptance.

Ron

Great Beginner

We sat down for his second trumpet lesson, the bright-eyed little eight-year-old boy and I. Last week I had shown him how to hold the horn, form his embouchure (the positioning of his lips), breathe correctly, produce a tone, and press the three trumpet valves correctly, so as to play *Old McDonald Had a Farm*. Last week, on the first try, he was able to do it.

He said he had worked hard all week on *Old McDonald*, and wanted to play it for me, first thing.

He played it... kind of. The rhythm was correct, but he neglected to use the valves. The trumpet is basically a composite set of bugles. It needs the valve combinations to play anything other than bugle calls. His *Old McDonald* was a stream of blurred noises, in the rhythm of *Old McDonald*.

I said, "You know, you'll never be a great trumpet player without learning how to use the valves."

Spontaneously, and with a big smile, he said, "Yeah, but I'm a great beginner!"

Patricia Lyon-Surrey Fine Art Photography

Thad

It's a crisp fall Monday morning as I turn off Old Route 11, onto the dirt drive leading past a few cows grazing on the other side of the rusting barbed wire. The small red barn is on the right, the weathered doublewide farmhouse is on the left. I have to drive very slowly as I approach the residence because Thor, a king-sized German shepherd, will bound out to greet me.

His wet nose is in my lap seconds after I crack open the truck door. I'm ready for him, Milkbone in hand, for our Monday morning ritual. He takes the treat and carelessly drops it on the ground. He's there for me, not for the Milkbone. He's several steps ahead as we approach the front door. He paws open the screen and nudges the main door with his nose.

Once inside he is met with a stern command to "Go Lie Down," which he reluctantly obeys, but only after he has nuzzled me one more time.

By the door, several pairs of old manure-covered rubber boots are grouped at attention, like old combat veterans in formation, praying not to be sent back into the muck of duty. Knickknack shelves share crowded wall space with a prized collection of framed chicken art. A dusty desk is stacked high with old financial papers and a dark blue baseball cap embroidered with "Jesus Is My Boss".

Two people wait for me, a man named Thad, dressed in farm-hand clothing, sitting in a worn, brown suede, overstuffed chair, and a warmly welcoming woman named Joanie, sitting on a black wooden stool beside him. Between them and the green collapsible canvas director's chair that I use, is a coffee-stained TV tray. A diminutive seven-year-old computer with two small bulbous speakers sits on the tray. There is a tiny blue light emanating from one of the speakers. It means that the speakers are turned on, waiting for our Facilitated Communication.

Thad is sitting directly across from me. He is forty-six, with bright eyes and a closely-trimmed white beard that gives him the appearance of a college professor. Thad has a profoundly autistic brain. For the last year he and I have worked together on psychological and social-developmental issues secondary to his autism. Our process is that I prompt him with questions and he types answers, one letter at a time, as Joanie, his Facilitated Communication aide, who is also his caregiver, guides his typing arm by gently touching his elbow. She supplies verbal encouragement as well. "Push through Thad. It's okay." A typical communication cycle takes 45 to 60 seconds. At the end of each cycle he presses a button, and the computer vocalizes what he has written with a clear monotone delivery. The only time the computer shows any emotion is when Thad has typed the word "very." The computer parrots back: "Very!"

Thad was misdiagnosed as mentally retarded for the first thirty-nine years of his life, primarily because he could not talk. He made lots of repetitive verbal noises, but no words. At age thirty-nine, Facilitated Communication was fully introduced to him, with his mother as his primary Facilitated Communication aide. At that time it was discovered that he was articulate, could speed-read, had an extensive vocabulary, could think abstractly, could manipulate his social milieu, and could do fairly complex mathematics in his head.

Now, seven years later, Thad is well advanced in all skill levels. He can write fiction as well as informative non-fiction essays. He speaks in simple sentences. His complex communication is all accomplished with computer-aided Facilitated Communication.

Two weeks ago his mother emotionally reported to me that he was in danger of losing an important opportunity, to be a contributing author to his social service agency's monthly newsletter. She said he was refusing to meet the submission deadline. This was curious to me, because he had consistently revealed to me that it was his intent to be a writer-activist, writing on behalf of the disabled of the world. I wondered what roadblock was keeping him from performing creatively in his stated field, and with his well-developed skills.

I asked him how often the newsletter was published. He slowly typed, "m-o-n-t-h-l-y." I asked him how long it typically would take to write a piece. He typed, "o-n-e o-r t-w-o d-a-y-s."

It was clear to me that meeting the deadline was not the problem. This was a performance problem.

I asked him to describe the person for whom he would be doing the writing. He typed that his agency case manager was going to "take away the opportunity" if he did not "show himself to be responsible" and "get down to business" and "grow up" and make the deadline.

I shifted the focus of our discussion. I asked him to describe helpful audience attitudes, paying close attention to those attitudes that would be personally helpful to him as he performed his writing. Thad typed out several attitudes including acceptance, forgiveness and appreciation. We also communicated about the unconditional form of each as the Ideal Audience form. We discussed how mental visual Cues work to prompt the helpful audience attitudes. We discussed the idea of performing (writing) *For* our chosen Social Audience, the people for whom our performance is a gift.

I listed the seven Masterful Life-Performance attitudes (Acceptance, Forgiveness, Trust, Empathy, Playfulness, Presence, and Appreciation) and asked him to name the Cues that came up for him. He typed, "M-o-m, J-o-a-n-i-e, J-e-n-n-y" (his mother, his caregiver, and his vocal and writing tutor). I asked him if he would consider firing his old audience. His face broke out in a wide grin. I asked him to consider writing *To* his new internal audience Cues, the three loving women he had mentioned, and *For* the disabled of the world. He typed out that he would consider doing it.

A week later I asked him how his writing was coming along. He typed, "o-k." I asked him if he had completed his piece. He typed, "Y-e-s. T-h-a-n-k-y-o-u f-o-r s-h-o-w-i-n-g m-e h-o-w t-o g-e-t b-e-y-o-n-d t-h-e r-o-a-d-b-l-o-c-k."

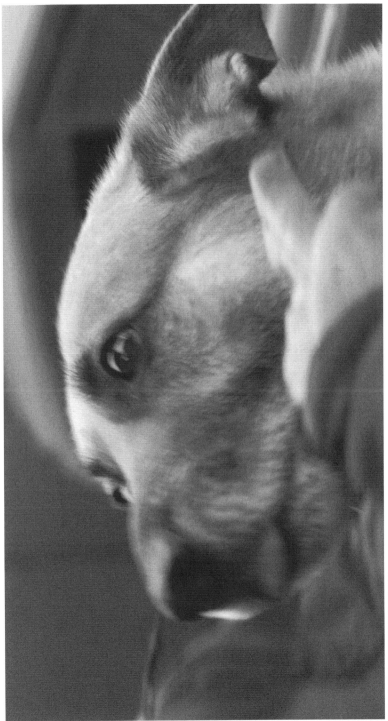

LETTER 27

Ron,

Thanks for talking about Unconditional Acceptance first. Coming from my perfectionistic background, I am beginning to see how I jump right in with immediate evaluations, usually negative, which is really nothing more than slapping conditions on whatever I'm doing.

When I was a kid, I was a lot more free to express myself, just like your young trumpet student. I was in the plays at school, and loved every minute of it.

I also like to think about how Unconditional Acceptance allows more information to come in. I close the judgment doors pretty fast on my own performances, slamming them shut with negative judgments. In considering medical interventions, I invite all the information I can about a case. I wouldn't think of being anything but open-minded. I'm devoted to best practice. The only time I practice Perfectionism at work is when I am evaluating my own work. That business about beating oneself up into perfection, that's me.

In your other story, the case manager was the source of the negative judgments. Once your client was given the insight and permission to get the case manager out of the picture, and focus on the unconditional acceptance of the women who love and support him, off he went.

I also like how you tie Unconditional Acceptance with Flow. I understand Flow. Been there, done that, a lot, and in many different areas. It's exciting to think I can move toward Flow by choosing my attitude. I have a lot of fun when I'm in a Flow state.

Please talk about another of your seven unconditional attitudes.

Evelyn

LETTER 28

Evelyn,

Thanks for your comments about Unconditional Acceptance. Kids are great teachers, aren't they?

And yes, Thad's internal transformation, and external performance, changed dramatically when he got in touch with the Unconditional Acceptance of his caregivers, the three women who loved him.

Next, I'd like to share some ideas about Unconditional Forgiveness.

Several of the Aramaic meanings of forgiveness are my favorites. In the Aramaic mind to forgive was to untie, set free, loosen, or let go, as one would untie oneself from cords to which one was previously bound. It is the "untie" and "set free" that I like best. I want to be set free to perform as I am able, not tied to any nonproductive, limiting condition.

Performing as a Perfectionist, I was tied to rigid unrealistic standards, which denied any probability of error. I was tied to a pattern of self-condemnation, anxiety, and sadness. This was my standard response to the inevitable presence of performance shortcomings and errors. As I chose the Excellist attitude of Unconditional Forgiveness, I began to untie myself from self-condemnation and the threat of self-condemnation. My anxiety diminished noticeably and I became more able to exercise the degree of risk associated with Flow. In my trumpet performances I became more accurate and more expressive. Peak Performance became the rule rather than the exception.

Evelyn, I have a story illustrating the power of Unconditional Forgiveness. It's about a team of highly talented and perfectionistic Little League baseball players. Enjoy.

Ron

Little League

After my Rotary meeting presentation on facilitating performance excellence using Masterful Life-Performance concepts, a fellow came up to me and asked if I would consider doing a performance coaching/training with his son's Little League team. They were in a slump. Even with lackluster playing, they had managed to win the state championship. They were the Lakeville, Minnesota (population 1,300) team. Apparently every kid who tried out for the team had been accepted. Now they were looking with trepidation at the next step, the Nationals in Kansas City. One chief concern was their scheduled game with the team from Orange County, California. The father told me that in Orange County 1,300 kids had tried out for the thirteen positions on the team. I agreed to do the talk after their next field workout.

I watched the hour-long workout, all the while talking with several of the coach-dads. These 10- to 12-year-old little kids were baseball machines. I had never seen that level of technical expertise in ones so young. I learned from the fathers that five of the players were super players (and super Perfectionists). If during a game they made a mistake, they were in the dumps for the remainder of the game. And the team was quick to follow the morose attitude of any of the five, thus spoiling the team performance for the rest of the game.

In preparation for the training I had visited the Nature Store at Mall of America, and purchased thirteen small stones embossed with Native American symbols. The only design for which thirteen were available was that of a snail. I bought them anyway.

After the workout, we all went into a large assembly room inside the school. Many of the parents attended, as well as the kids in their mud-stained uniforms. I opened with a compassionate yet authoritative voice. "Tonight I'm not going to talk about baseball. You are the baseball experts. That's clear to me after watching your workout. I'm going to talk to you about performance. Right now you think of yourselves as baseball players, performing baseball. When I finish tonight, my hope is that you will see yourselves as performers, playing baseball."

For the next hour I went on to cover the basics of Masterful Life-Performance: the essential nature of excellent technical form, the playing *For* others (in this case their teammates and parent supporters), the development of helpful inner-audience attitudes, the visualization of a helpful audience, the inviting of peak performance through the prompting of the internal audience Cue (performing *To* the internal audience Cue), the forgiveness response to errors made, the inevitability of error in performance.

Surprisingly, these young kids seemed to get it. Most were quietly attentive. Some asked questions: "What do I do when I make a big mistake? I don't want to let my parents down." "What do I do with bad feelings? I'm scared of Orange County... the Nationals... of making a mistake."

At the end of the evening I asked them to line up side-by-side. I gave each a snail stone. I invited the player on the far left to look into the eyes of the player next to him and say: "I forgive any mistake, small or big, that you make at Kansas City." And then click the snail stones together as a sign of sealing the pact. Then move to the next player to the right. In turn each player would do this with each other player, until all players had click-sealed the commitment.

I suggested that each player slip the small snail stone in the pocket of his uniform as a reminder during play. My curiosity was at full bore ten days later when they had returned from Kansas City. I called the dad who had contacted me to meet with them.

I heard his joyful proud voice say: "They lost to Orange County... 14 to 12. They outplayed themselves at every game. They were so proud. They were ranked nineteenth in small town teams across the nation."

Patricia Lyon-Surrey Fine Art Photography

LETTER 29

Ron,

I can just see them, out there on the brightly lit manicured ball field. Fledgling Major Leaguers, in their Lakeville uniforms, their last names in large black letters on the back. Energized with every small victory. Feeling the smooth hard bulge of their pocketed snail stones, cuing up forgiveness every time things didn't go quite right. Every time a teammate made a mistake. Every time THEY made a mistake. Their fear discharged like a load of gravel off a dump truck, as they realized that the kids from Orange County were every bit as vulnerable. Now they could play anticipating the forgiveness of their teammates, and focus their youthful exuberance on the game. Very Cool!

Keep going Ron. The theoretical part of your letters is helpful, but I really love the stories best.

Evelyn

LETTER 30

Evelyn,

There is no movement in human behavior, no risk, and no creative change without the attitudinal field of Trust being present. Without sufficient Trust we stay in our little behavioral caves, not venturing out to play. Before we venture out, we need reassurance that we can handle the territory ahead. Performance requires movement. Trusting attitude is a necessary condition to invite movement, and most certainly a precondition of peak performance.

The attitudes of the Ideal Audience are particularly helpful if the primary threat of loss has to do with the loss of self-esteem. I am convinced that the risk-related threats of most performance scenarios have as their theme loss of self-esteem, and the desire to avoid the accompanying sadness. I am remembering that sadness is associated with loss. We risk being subjected to the self-induced emotional pain of sadness when we step out of our comfort zone. Ideal Audience attitudes act as an emotional safety net.

Also, once an error has been made, Unconditional Trust (in tandem with the other Ideal Audience attitudes) acts like a trampoline, providing resilience and quicker recovery. Excellists might fall, but are caught by the trampoline of Trust and bounce back.

Evelyn, I've included two stories illustrating high-risk scenarios. The first has to do with risk of physical pain, and the second has to do with risk of social embarrassment and potential loss of self-esteem.

Thanks for your encouraging words. I like the stories best too.

Ron

No

Gripping the walker with more survival instinct than physical strength, I made it back to the hospital bed, and sat on its side trying not to rumple the gown under me. Even slight folds were an intolerable irritation, adding to the pain coming from the surgical site. This time I'd gone out ten feet and back. It was my second walk of the day, having endured a two-hour major abdominal surgery that morning, and a first walk with a round trip of under four feet.

Sternly, my newly assigned nurse said, "Okay, it's time to get back into the bed. You lean back. I'll grab your legs, and in one quick move we'll swing you back in."

Through the disorienting trauma, and the daze of the narcotics, I said, "No."

With irritation in her voice she said, "What?"

I said, "No. I'll direct."

I knew what she didn't know. I had gotten myself in and out of the bed that morning, with minimal help, and without extra pain. It had just taken me a long time. I glanced at the clock on the wall. 1:02. I ordered, "Just put your arm out. Don't pull. Don't push. I'll do the work." I knew that there was nothing wrong with my arms. If I transferred all the tension to them, and away from my severed abdominal muscles, I'd make it just fine. I wasted no trust on her. I trusted myself, my I'm-still-in-charge-medication-fogged-up-survival self.

Imperceptibly, we began to move. She kept trying to speed up the process. I commanded, "Don't push. I'll do the tension."

She grew more impatient. Our ultra-slow-dance continued. Finally my head graced the pillows of the upright back of the hospital bed. Victory! No Added Pain! I glanced at the clock. 1:10. It had taken eight minutes to lie down in bed. She left in a huff. I overheard her sharp remark to my wife Maggie just outside the door. "Is he always like that?" Maggie burst into tears.

Weeks later we humored over coffee at Capitol Grounds, our favorite coffee-house sanctuary. We replayed the scene, coming up with clever responses to the insensitive question.

"No... only when he has a fresh eleven-inch incision, extending the full length of his abdominal cavity, held together by thirty-eight staples."

"No... only on days he's just had his spleen, two-thirds of his stomach, and a cancerous tumor the size of a grapefruit surgically removed."

Together we sipped and we laughed.

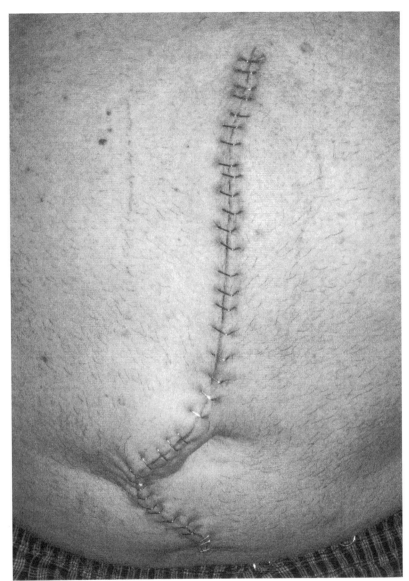

Charlie

It's been years since that phone call with Charlie. It came precisely at the time that I was piecing together the list of helpful Unconditional Attitudes of one's Ideal Interior Audience. My friend and one of my trumpet performance mentors, Charles Schlueter, was the longest seated Principal Trumpet of the Boston Symphony Orchestra (25 years) before he retired in 2006.

"Ron, you'll never guess what note I missed last week at Tanglewood."

"Oh no, Charlie, what?"

Some explanation is due here. In addition to being unquestionably a world-class symphonic trumpeter, Charlie earned a reputation for taking performance risks. Simply stated, he pushed the trumpet to the limit, and well beyond the limit of most players. Whether it meant playing louder, softer, more lyrical, or more forceful, there was the bell of Charlie's trumpet pointed directly over the music stand, and never into the stand, unless the music specifically called for it.

"Well... you know the forte solo low C in *Petrouchka*?"

"Sure."

"I missed it... I didn't just miss it... I REALLY MISSED IT!"

Now I was riveted to this conversation. Low C is the easiest note on the trumpet. It is the first pitch that comes out of the instrument when a beginning player lifts the trumpet to the lips. Charlie was telling me that he had made one of the loudest unexpected mistakes in the orchestral repertoire, and he had sprayed this THING all over the Boston Symphony and the 5,000 in attendance at the Tanglewood concert. This was a mistake that could reduce anybody but a Masterful Performer to tears, and certainly ruin the rest of one's performance. Also this low C is followed a few seconds later by a delicate lyrical cornet solo that is of sufficient difficulty to warrant it being in most orchestral auditions. Being the curious performance psychologist, I quickly asked: "What did you do? How did you react?"

"Well Ron, I had to fight the urge to slap my knee and laugh out loud. It was the funniest goddamned thing that ever happened to me! The other trumpets were just holding it in too."

"Charlie, what about the cornet solo?!"

"Oh... no sweat."

Supreme confidence is what he called it. I was thinking supreme Trust with a generous dose of supreme Playful Humor. Within a few seconds Charlie's Interior Audience had supplied him with the helpful attitudes of Trust and Playful Humor, and the accompanying resiliency, allowing him to perform a delicate difficult solo after a really big bomb of a mistake.

Ron and Charlie, International Trumpet Guild Conference 1985, Albuquerque, New Mexico

Image Reproduction Patricia Lyon-Surrey Fine Art Photography

LETTER 31

Ron,

Being a surgeon, *No* was a bit of a wakeup call! In the profession, we can get emotionally hardened when we deal with the pain of others day-in and day-out. I respect patients like you, but there are some that are just plain difficult.

I admire the quality of self-trust, and think of it as contributing to one's courage. *No* is a clear example of both.

Charlie was something else, making a mistake like that in front of so many learned people, and then recovering so quickly. Truly the mark of a master performer. Your friend has amazing resilience. I see why you have such strong regard for him, and why you paid so much attention to his performance process.

Both of you have learned to trust yourselves when faced with difficult circumstances. I see why you have listed Unconditional Trust as one of your Ideal Audience attitudes.

Keep going. What's next?

Evelyn

LETTER 32

Evelyn,

Unconditional Empathy is next.

I think of empathy, and experience it, as multidimensional understanding. The three dimensions that stand out for me are intellectual understanding (what the performer is doing), emotional understanding (what the performer is feeling), and understanding of intent (what personal and social goals the performer is intending to accomplish, and what universal human needs the performer is attempting to satisfy). In its unconditional state, there can be no circumstance in which empathy is not fully present.

In all complex, highly refined performance, preparation consists of thousands of hours of practiced study. We the observers see a performance snapshot, not the epic movie behind the single frame. When we are privy to the backstory, we begin to build empathy for the technical challenges being faced, the technical expertise displayed, the emotions rippling through the performer, the degree of emotional regulation needed, and the depth and nature of personal and social need which motivates the performer to satisfy.

Masterful Life-Performance is about developing these dimensions of understanding within ourselves, for our own performances, and for those of others. With respect to the performance needs of others, Masterful Life-Performance is aligned with the Arabian proverb: "Because I have been athirst, I will dig a well that others may drink."

Is it reasonable to conclude that we are the only ones who have experienced the entire backstory of our own performances? Are we the most qualified source, and potentially the most unconditional source, of empathic self-understanding? Are we the only ones who have lived through, and are living through, our own entire performance drama? My answer to these questions is a hearty Yes.

So Evelyn, I am encouraging you to continue being curious about the technical aspects of your performances, fully embrace and honor the accompanying emotions that wash over you as you perform, and make the attempt to list the personal and social needs you intend to satisfy.

To this end I have included two stories, one that illustrates the presence of empathy, and the other in which empathy is temporarily overlooked.

Ron

Escape

Tran was a minute Vietnamese man, a mesh of black hair, sinewy thin arms and spindly legs. His back had a curvature so severe that at first sight I thought I was looking at a giant insect. How he had found his way to this inner-city residential facility for impoverished and mentally disabled adult males was a mystery. Recently hired as the Social Services Coordinator of the one hundred-bed facility, I found his case the most troubling of all.

The story that followed him was that, at one time, he was a high-ranking member of the Vietnamese judiciary. He had been taken prisoner by the Viet Cong, and placed in a two-by-two-by-four foot cage where he remained for eleven years. In the eleventh year of his captivity he had escaped and become a boat person, eventually making it to the United States. His tortured time in captivity had robbed him of his sanity and physical integrity.

He had been given a third-floor room in this aging residential facility. The two windows in the room were laced with flat plank makeshift wooden bars apparently designed for his safety.

After visiting him, and observing him move as a spider would move, scampering on all fours across the floor and, with measured agility, up the wall around the barred windows, I became concerned for his wellbeing. Given his reported history, it seemed apparent to me that Tran had only one psychological goal: escape. My intuition told me that it was just a matter of time before he would go out a window. I argued to have him moved to the first floor, to no avail.

Three weeks later, as I drove into the parking lot, I noticed a crowd gathered around a small black human blob, in a graveled area close to the building. I knew in flash that Tran had escaped. I was certain that the three-story fall had killed him.

Not so. He had bounced off a car hood onto the gravel. I was elated to learn that the entire extent of his injury was a single broken ankle.

Again my argument surfaced. This time he was moved, not to the first floor, but to a safe-room hospital facility, with round-the-clock care including daily visits from a Vietnamese gentleman, who spoke to him softly in his native tongue and brought him lusciously fragrant Vietnamese home cooking.

Patricia Lyon-Surrey Fine Art Photography

Casino

Driving across the vast Southwest on a monotonous, hot mirage of a highway is about as interesting as watching railroad tracks paralleling into the horizon, never touching each other.

The irritation of boredom is compounded when you are hungry.

"Maggie, how far 'til Las Vegas?"

My wife says, "Forty-seven miles. It's worth the wait. The casino food is good, and it's cheap."

I'm thinking that the casinos use their cheap food to lure you into their gambling lairs, to suck your money away.

Later, as I push away from the table, my mood is completely changed. I'm finding that Caesar's Whatever-They-Call-It is really quite interesting.

The café is perched on the level just above the palatial gambling den. Rows of slot machines, blackjack tables, and roulette wheels are populated by mesmerized, quasi-busy, anxiously dazed gamblers.

We've just finished a huge, cheap meal. It's time to get back on the road.

Just as I take my first wide stride down the broad, thickly carpeted stairway emptying into the cavernous casino, I let go with the loudest, longest, uncontrolled methane moment of my life.

I'm shocked into disbelief. Plunged into humiliation, I imagine that I have just shut down the entire casino. All those mesmerized, half-alive gamblers are suddenly wide-eyed alert, staring directly at me.

All I want to do is grab Maggie's hand and run for the door.

Then, in a loud voice she says: "Ronny, do you know what you just did?"

Patricia Lyon-Surrey Fine Art Photography

LETTER 33

Ron,

Thanks for your letter and stories about Empathy. It is such an important part of my process as a surgeon. I don't think I could carry out the procedures I do without having a strong empathic understanding of my patients' conditions, and my intent to help them. And I really like your emphasis on our being the most qualified source of Empathy for ourselves. Yes, we're the only ones who have experienced and endured the totality our own life performance experiences. I'm beginning to see how I can be a helpful audience to myself. Maybe even my best audience.

As for Tran, the lives of torture victims are heroic examples of the human will to live. His life story, even as fragmented and partial as you present it, brings a perspective to me that profoundly shrinks the severity of my own emotional challenges.

Thank God for caregivers like the Vietnamese gentleman you mentioned. I can smell the aroma of the love food.

As for your performance (if you want to call it that) in the casino, Maggie's response certainly showed a lapse in Empathy. I suspect she was as shocked and surprised as you were. I think I would have been knocked off-balance too. I bet you both still have a good laugh from time to time over that one.

More please.

Evelyn

LETTER 34

Evelyn,

Since the casino incident, the question, "Do you know what you just did?" is our family's standard response to an obvious faux pas.

Now, onto one of my favorite audience attitudes: Unconditional Playfulness, and its sidekick, Humor.

I think of Playful Humor as the lubricant of performance. It loosens up everything. It reduces the emotional tension, and allows us to get back into the emotional zone associated with performance excellence and peak performance. I suppose if Playful Humor were a color it would be bright yellow. But then again it could be pitch black. Whatever catches us off guard and interjects the humorous surprise. I have included three stories, each illustrating Unconditional Playfulness. In all three circumstances Playful Humor makes its unlikely presence known.

Enjoy.

Ron

Swedish Fish

After a full day of doing psychotherapy, listening to desperate non-empathic stories, I was in a state of sad irritation. The need for empathic understanding is the most crying need of the human race, empathy being in chronic short supply. Acknowledging that I am in the same emotional bread line with everyone else, I decided I needed some nurturing, and as always, I turned to food. More precisely, candy. Even more precisely, red gummy Swedish Fish.

I drove past my home, and over another two miles of back roads, to the Adamant Co-op Store, the oldest co-op in Vermont, all 225 square feet of it, including the post office and the post boxes. This was a big year in its long history. They boarded up the outside privy with its bucket of lime next to the one-holer, and added an inside toilet. They built a new kitchen upstairs so the cook could supply fresh bakery goods. And the real big twenty-first century step was a credit card machine.

So as I have done from time to time, especially after a hard day, I drove over to hang out, look at the organic products on the couple of shelves, get out of the winter chill and read the wine bottle labels. I wish I liked wine. I do to a point, but it leaves me uncomfortable, a bit shamed at the cost, and slightly depressed the next day. By contrast, Swedish Fish leave me slightly uncomfortable, without shame at the cost (one cent per fish) and without depression the next day.

So I went over to the jar on the candy shelf, counted out my usual fifty, and put them in the little waxed paper bag provided. Dropping the bag on the wooden counter, I told the lady by the old cash register and the new credit card machine that I needed them for their omega-3 fatty acid content.

She said, "What?"

I said, "Omega-3 fatty acid, after all, they're fish."

She said, "What?"

I said, "It's just a joke."

She said, "It's pretty bad when you have to explain a joke."

I said, "Yes. Dissecting a joke is like dissecting a frog. It just doesn't work when you try to put it back together."

She said, "What?"

I gave her the fifty cents. She asked me if I lived around there. I was surprised. I'd seen her at the co-op for a long time. I said I lived on Lightening Ridge Road.

"Where on Lightening Ridge?" she asked.

Lightening Ridge Road is two miles long, and has about two-dozen houses, two dairy farms, and an elementary school.

I said, "Just beyond the elementary school, on Deerwillow Farm, in the red farmhouse... the old Harding Place." She said that she pays no attention to the color of houses.

"I hear there's a new bathroom here in the store," I said.

She said, "Yes."

"Could I use it?"

She said, "It's only for the staff. It's a chemical toilet."

I looked around. She was the only staff in the store.

"Oh," I said.

I was feeling a lot of pressure by then. I considered telling her, very matter-of-factly, that I'd just have to take my Swedish Fish and my pee and go home. And then watch her face.

Then, I figured she would just say, "What?"

So I took the Swedish Fish and my full bladder, and drove the icy back road, carefully avoiding the bumps and winter potholes. By the time I got home I had eaten all fifty, and was feeling a nice gentle sense of discomfort.

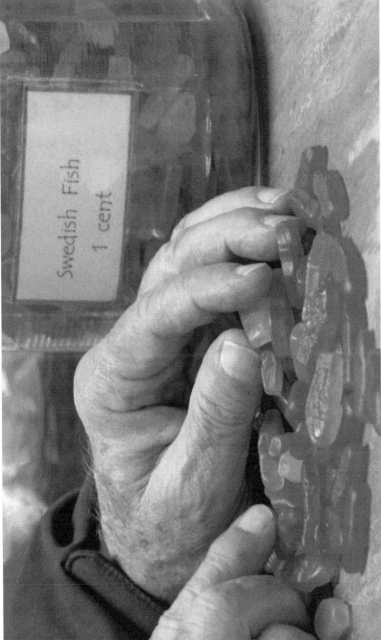

Harold

Humor is the great bridge to our mutual humanity, working its wonders, weaving its whimsy and surprise.

Recently graduated, and with my counseling psychology degree in hand, I faced a tough job market. Finally I found a job at an inner-city residential facility that housed impoverished and mentally disordered adult males. I was to be their Social Services Coordinator.

There was no written job description. After a short interview, the director hired me on the spot. I was told that each of the one hundred or so residents had multiple diagnoses. I was to be their mental health counselor, and work to keep the facility "peaceful and safe."

During my first week I got a call from the director. Two roommate residents were screaming obscenities at each other, both highly agitated. He said, "Oh, by the way, Harold has Huntington's Disease. Come down and take care of this, will you?"

Huntington's Disease is a rare, inherited condition, in which the neurons of the brain degenerate, leading to jerky uncontrolled movements, clumsiness, facial grimaces, and twitches.

Sure enough, both men were exploding threats and obscenities at each other. Mediation was out of the question. After a few moments of watching, and waiting for a break in the barrage, I looked directly into Harold's eyes and gently said, "Hey, how about coming with me?"

Miraculously, and clumsily, he followed me down the hall to my tiny office, mumbling obscenities all the way.

He had a tough time keeping his body in my client chair. His whole being seemed out of control. Simultaneously, his diseased body and troubled mind fed his verbal rage, all directed toward his roommate.

Again, I watched and waited. Finally a break. "Tell me what your roommate did to you."

"The son-of-a-bitch stole my cigarettes... and my cologne... and lied to me."

Again I waited.

"But I got him back." He said with the hint of a grin.

"Oh?"

"Yeh, I came in. He was sleepin', with the fan blowin' on his head. I pissed right into the fan."

I looked at Harold and dissolved into uncontrolled laughter. Tears streamed down my face as I slid off my chair onto the floor. I don't know how long I was down there, but when I managed to make it back onto my chair, wiping my face, I looked over at Harold's calm wide grin. He was settled, and we were friends from then on.

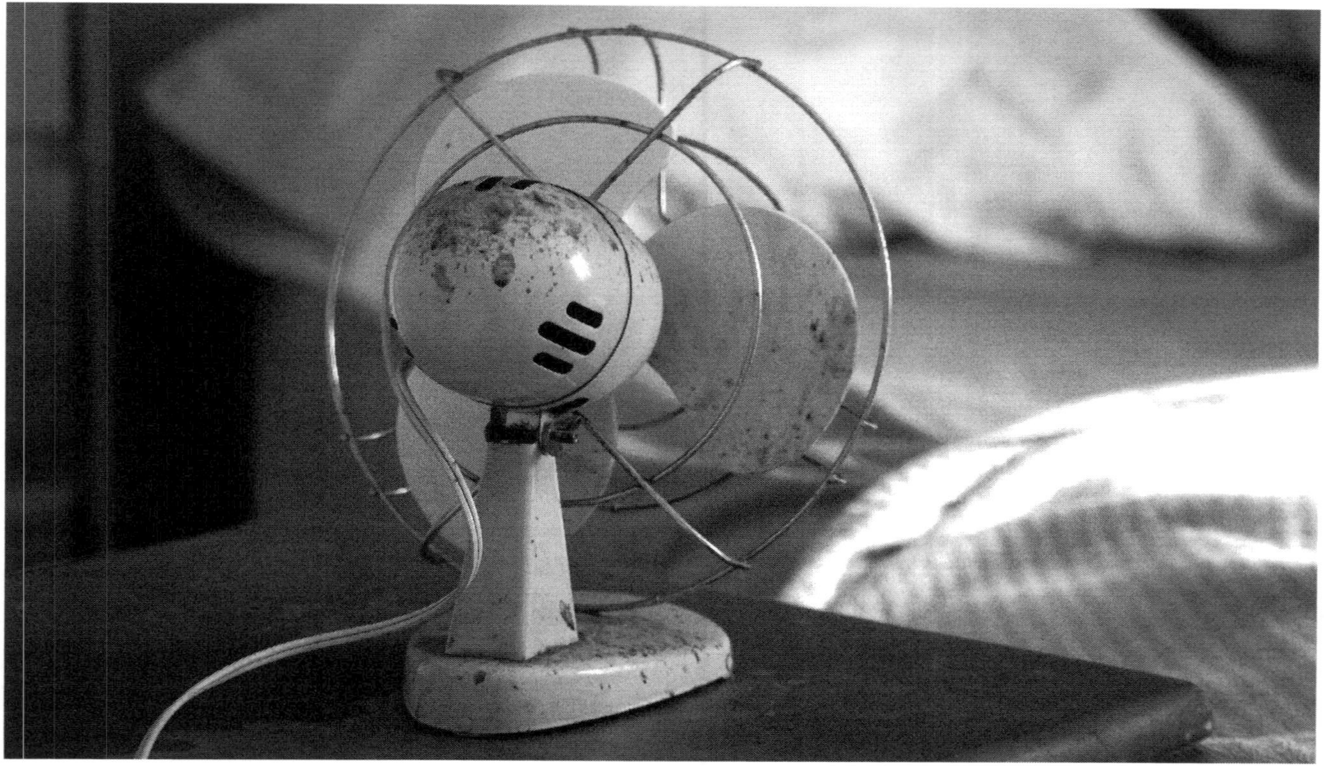

Patricia Lyon-Surrey Fine Art Photography

A Philosophical Conversation

So there we were, my wife and I, driving up Towne Hill Road past the cornfields to our Friday morning writing class. I dominated the conversation.

"I think a person's vision of God is the most important choice made in life. Why, it is the genesis from which all personal values and subsequent behaviors spring."

The three-car traffic ahead slowed a bit.

"Imagine how a personal, loving vision of God influences our sense of security in this vast otherwise impersonal universe. How it works to overcome existential isolation and aloneness. I agree with Viktor Frankl, that choice is paramount."

Maggie said, "That's a load of shit."

I said, "What?"

She said, "Look up there. We're following one of those poop-caked, manure spreader tanker trucks."

Patricia Lyon-Surrey Fine Art Photography

Ron,

All I have to say is that Maggie's timing is impeccable, as is her mindfulness. There she is, living in the present. And you? Obviously in a philosophical flow-state. What a pair! I'd love to be a mouse in your house, or a fly on the wall, and get to listen to more of your conversations. Knowing you both, I bet the parallel-universe ones are rare.

And as for Harold, I would have been right down there on the floor with you, laughing ourselves silly. What a guy. And what challenges life has dealt him.

I have a confession. My equivalent to your Swedish Fish is Jelly Bellies. I keep a jar in my office at work and one at home in my study. I've been known to overdo and regret the mild nausea. Oh well. Sometimes the nausea risk is just worth it.

I see why Unconditional Playfulness/Humor made your helpful attitude list. I use it all the time to trim off my excess emotional tension. After having these exchanges with you, I'll use it more.

I've been keeping a list of your chosen helpful performance attitudes. According to my list Unconditional Presence is next.

You've got my full interest. Have at it.

Evelyn

LETTER 36

Evelyn,

I don't recommend being either a mouse in our house or a fly on the wall. We have two cats, Coffee Bean and Callie Cat, both hunters. And one of my several compulsivities is swatting the cluster flies that are so prevalent in our old Vermont farmhouse. Since you're considered family, you have a standing invitation to visit anytime, and you can be assured that Maggie and I will not change our communication patterns in your presence. Speaking of presence, you are correct about Unconditional Presence being next.

I have found Unconditional Presence to be an exceedingly powerful attitude, as well as a powerful facilitator of attitudes. I think of it as unique in this respect. It has a dual role. It is an attitude itself, a state of mind, and it also carries with it a unique constellation of embedded attitudes. It is like a light source that delivers a rainbow spectrum of discrete colors. When I'm performing I'm constantly making choices. I think of Presence as the attitude delivery system from my Audience to my choice-making performing Self. I like to call the choice-making component of Self my Internal Performer. The performance metaphor on which Masterful Life-Performance is built holds that the Internal Performer chooses, the Audience is the source of attitude, and Presence delivers attitude.

I find myself imagining living with an internal state of being where life-affirming attitudes are always available, a state of Unconditional Presence. Note that the adverb "always" denotes unconditionality. I am "always" free to choose the focus of my consciousness in such a way as to prompt life-affirming attitudes. In my imaginings there is no condition or circumstance in which I can be separated from my chosen life-affirming attitudes. I am "always" free to choose the attitude with which I respond to circumstance. There is no separation from helpful attitude, as long as my consciousness is intact and I imagine I can choose.

My thinking prompts Unconditional Presence, primarily by

visualizing my chosen Internal Audience Cue. The Cue is a powerful prompt because experience has taught me to associate it with unconditional and life-affirming attitudes. It can be called into mind anytime I choose, and can remain as long as I exercise conscious choice.

At various times I have thought of the Cue as a key, which allows a door to be opened, thus revealing the unconditional attitudes beyond. Also I have thought of it as the door itself. Whatever metaphor I use, the primary function of the Cue is to prompt unconditionally loving Presence into my consciousness, and with it, helpful attitudes and emotional regulation.

It is important to distinguish between the Cue and the helpful attitudes associated with the Cue, of which Unconditional Presence and Unconditional Forgiveness are two examples. The Cue is not the attitude. The Cue is the prompt. What is fascinating to me is that there exists a relatively small number of essential attitudes that invite Masterful Performance, and an almost infinite variety of Cues that invite the helpful attitudes.

Here's a sampling of personal Cues that people have mentioned to me:

Grampa Red
My horse, Zoya
Jesus
Champo the dog
Dad
Butterflies
Family
My wife's face
Buddha
Friends
My teacher
Mom
Pine needles warming in the sun
Susie the cow
Church sanctuary

Mountain path
God
Disabled child
My mentor
Painting of an old man wrapped in a quilt
Sunlight sparkling on windswept waters
A stand of sugar maples

As you can readily see, the Cues are as varied as the private life experiences of each person. Our commonality is found in the few helpful attitudes. Living with a few helpful attitudes is a universal human need. The Cues and behaviors by which we invite the attitudes into our performances are as varied and complex as our life experiences, and our genetic, social and cultural inheritance.

Let me summarize.

Our Internal Performer chooses the Cue. The Cue prompts Unconditional Presence and its accompanying helpful attitudes. The attitudes facilitate helpful emotions and emotional regulation. When our emotions are helpful and regulated (that is, matched in intensity to the task at hand), the likelihood of functional excellence in performance is enhanced. Thus, we love ourselves into excellence. With practice, Masterful Performance becomes like a well-rehearsed virtuosic orchestra. It is dependable, responsive, and delivers a beautiful experience.

I have included three stories, each of which illustrate the power of Unconditional Presence through the judicious choice of an Audience Cue. The first, *Brother Lawrence*, comes from a classic piece of writing on Christian spirituality. The second, *Nursing Home*, is my recollection of one of my own trumpet performances. The third, *Cuz*, is a reflection on the life of my cousin, Sally Thurston.

Please note the wide variance of the Cues and the commonality of helpful attitudes prompted.

Ron

Brother Lawrence

There, silhouetted against the snow, was a dry and leafless tree. The boy's eyes were transfixed, as was his whole being. As he contemplated the changes that the coming spring would bring, he was overtaken by an overwhelming and loving Presence, which he interpreted as God. From that time forth he constantly sought to "walk in His presence." That was in 1629. Thirty-seven years later, after repeated bumblings, accidents and failures of accomplishment, Nicholas Herman entered the Carmelite Order in Paris as a lay brother, Brother Lawrence. Within the monastery walls he became the Order's cook and kitchen cleanup person. Both within and outside those walls, Brother Lawrence also became a primary source of inspiration and spiritual direction for all who knew him.

The Practice of the Presence of God is a collection of his letters and reported conversations preserved shortly after his death at age 80. They demonstrate how he used loving attitudes, as cued by his vision of God, to bring about positive emotional transformation in his own life and in the lives of others. Sadness and anxiety were the emotions neutralized by his spiritual discipline.

Two short excerpts summarize the internal transformation and spiritual discipline of Brother Lawrence:

> *That he had been long troubled in mind from a certain belief that he should be damned; that all the men in the world could not have persuaded him to the contrary; but that he had thus reasoned with himself about it: "I did not engage in a religious life but for the love of God, and I have endeavoured to act only for Him."* [14]

> *I have quitted all forms of devotion and set prayers but those to which my state obliges me. And make it my business only to persevere in His holy presence, wherein I keep myself by a simple attention and a general fond regard for God; or, to speak better,*

an habitual, silent, and secret conversation of the soul with God, which often causes me joys and raptures inwardly, and sometimes outwardly, so great that I am forced to use means to moderate them and prevent their appearance to others." [56]

Thus Brother Lawrence exercised his unusual ability to use his love-based spiritual discipline to dissolve the harmful emotions caused by his previous pathological thinking, and supplant them with profound gladness.

Patricia Lyon-Surrey Fine Art Photography

Nursing Home

They're being brought in, one by one, to the frilly curtained, institutional gray activity room, sunken into their wheelchairs, none of them seemingly present. About half of the two-dozen elderly ladies arrive with their eyes open. Some of the eyes are filled with bewilderment, some blank, having no remaining emotional reflection. The eyes of the rest are gently closed, accessories on expressionless faces. Their white-haired heads bob a bit as the assistants line up the wheelchairs for my trumpet presentation. There's one elderly gentleman, the last to arrive. Then the doors are closed, to mute the distant kitchen noise.

I'm here to do an "Informance," an introduction to the upcoming Santa Barbara Symphony concert, my first such presentation in a nursing home setting. Informances are a reach-out program of the orchestra. Free tickets are available to all who can make the journey to the concert hall. I'm here to talk about the program and play my trumpet. The instructions are to play anything that might entertain the residents.

As I begin my solo performance, I realize that something is missing. There's no social audience. I'm thinking nobody's home out there. How can I perform to a nonpresent audience?

I go ahead anyway, with a few concert orchestral trumpet excerpts. I talk aloud between solos. I perform to my Internal Audience. This process begins to set me free to be more curious about the people in front of me.

I begin thinking about the ages of these folks. They were young adults during the Swing Era, the time of the Big Bands: Benny Goodman, Glen Miller and the Dorsey Brothers. I know all that music from my high school jazz band days.

Casting concert excerpts aside, I let out with the adlib solos of Harry James and Ziggy Elman, two trumpet superstars of the era, *A String of Pearls... Tenderly... Stardust... And the Angels Sing*. And then I'm done.

A soft patter of applause from the nursing assistants is accompanied by silence from those in the wheelchairs. I put my silver trumpet back into its glove-leather case.

Just as I open the door to leave, a nurse pulls me aside, and says: "Did you see the expression on the face of the gentleman over on the end? When you played *And the Angels Sing*, he broke out in a wide grin. It's the first time I've seen him smile in six months."

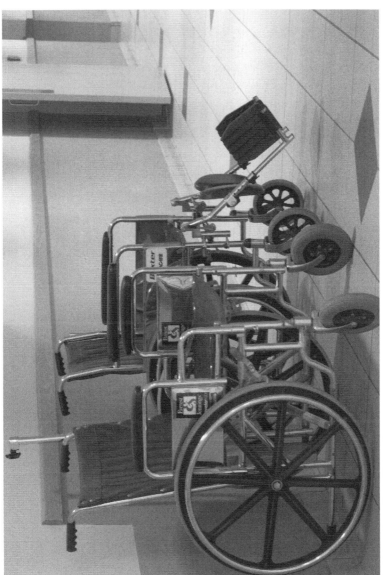

Cuz

Sally called me Cuz. She died a quiet death, late on a Wednesday night. She had just finished a crossword puzzle, and then lay back on her pillow, with her glasses still on. She was sixty-eight. I was sixty-nine. She wasn't supposed to live this long.

Some of my earliest memories are of family holidays and camping vacations, where she and I experienced a truly loving family. There were squeals of excitement when we initially met after the long car trip between California and Washington State. Christmas presents were opened on Christmas Eve. There was way too much childhood excitement to wait until morning. Camping on Puget Sound included freshly gathered clams and oysters bubbling on the campfire grill, smothered with butter. Our parents played rubber after rubber of bridge, with martinis at five o'clock.

I was present in our kitchen when my folks received my aunt and uncle's letter telling of Sally's diagnosis of diabetes and the prognosis. She was four at the time, and was given five years to live. A temporary cure for diabetes had been discovered in 1945. Sally's insulin shots began in 1947. I was shocked and confused. What do you mean, getting shots with needles every day? What do you mean, not being able to eat candy?

By age 14, Sally's condition had taken hold of her life. She was an emaciated adolescent with few friends and a huge library of books lining the walls of her bedroom.

The word "library" became of critical importance to her at an early age, and her long career as a librarian was the staple nutrient keeping her meager self-esteem alive. The literary world was her world. She was powerful and competent in that world.

Teddy bears were her Cue to Unconditional Love. Winnie The Pooh was Sally's favorite children's book character. During a visit to Vermont, I took her to the Vermont Teddy Bear Factory, and then to the Barre Sculpture Studio of Jerry Williams, an acquaintance of mine, and a world-renowned sculptor of granite teddy bears. Some of his creations are fifteen feet tall, weigh tons, and present with a realism as if they had just come out of Sally's bedroom.

Sally and Jerry were soul mates. I left them alone to talk teddy bear talk. The granite bears came alive that afternoon. So did Sally.

For many years our contact had been through her late-night phone calls, generally when I was bleary-eyed. Sight gone in her right eye, injuries to ankles and knees from falls, six needles of insulin every day, chronic major depression, social conflict galore, and reports about a trip to England to buy another special teddy bear. Or more often, no news at all. Just hearing my voice and knowing I heard hers.

Winnie The Pooh understood:

Piglet sided up to Pooh from behind. "Pooh?" he whispered.

"Yes, Piglet?"

"Nothing," said Piglet, taking Pooh's paw. "I just wanted to make sure of you."

Image Reproduction Patricia Lyon-Surrey Fine Art Photography

Ron,

After reading your latest letter and the three stories, several things struck me. The first was how important Cues are to people. They use them over and over, to get in touch with the attitudes they associate with them. Your cousin loved her bears and no doubt had a large collection. Brother Lawrence loved his vision of God and turned that love into a spiritual practice that changed his life for the better. And the elderly gentleman must have listened to a lot of swing music in his lifetime. Lots of smiles there. Lots of loving presence.

Also I was struck by the wide variety of Cues through which Unconditional Presence was actualized. Teddy bears, theology, swing music. What a spread!

I have to admit that I had flashbacks of my Intro to Psychology class and what I learned about the classical conditioning of emotional-behavioral responses. You can bet that Pavlov's dog experienced an emotional trigger when the bell went off. Cues can be powerful stimuli.

When I think about the three examples, my imagination is in high gear. If this powerful Cue process works so well to change and regulate emotion, why not use it any time I want, and especially in emotionally challenging circumstances?

I think that Masterful Life-Performance, used at will, qualifies as a spiritual practice. Do you agree? And if it works well, what would keep me from using it any time I need to deal with my runaway emotions?

Evelyn

LETTER 38

Evelyn,

Because I equate the concepts of spirit and attitude, I agree with you that Masterful Life-Performance is a spiritual practice. Certainly I practice it, and have for years. Lots of repetitions. Lots of conscious choice making. Lots of using it as a path to increased emotional well-being, and excellence in performance.

With regard to your behavioral psychology observation, ML-P uses the classical conditioning already established in the performer. Helpful attitudes, and the accompanying emotional regulation, are prompted by the Ideal Audience Cue, just like the conditioned salivation response of Pavlov's dog. (I apologize for the somewhat disgusting parallel.)

Because I have noticed that peak performances come more often when I *invite* them using ML-P, I keep growing in my devotion to the process. The behaviorists would say that the increase in the peak performances itself reinforces my behavior. They would also say that the random nature of the peak performance occurrence is highly reinforcing as well.

I have no problem with using behavioristic concepts, except when they are used as absolute predictors of outcomes. Performance outcome (product), especially that associated with peak performance, is the result of the mingling of highly complex processes. I believe it is helpful to acknowledge how truly complex performance is, and that any attempt to describe it, including ML-P, is partial. Therefore the interior process that I use throughout the before-during-after-performance cycle is meant to *invite* excellence. My preference is to approach performance with the macro-attitude of open-minded humility. My intent is to *invite, not control* outcomes.

When I'm in Flow, I experience the most control, and the fear of losing control is at an ebb. When I'm out of the creative state of Flow, the great temptation is to put control at the top of my goal list, and step away from the very process that produces the excellence I want.

The masterful performers I know or have studied, put process first. They understand that excellence in process comes before excellence in product.

Evelyn, thanks for your insightful responses. Right now I'd like to continue talking about the unconditional attitudes that I have singled out as critical to the Masterful Life-Performance process. The seventh, and last, is Unconditional Appreciation, the attitude of gratitude.

Unconditional Appreciation has found its valued position in the ML-P constellation of helpful, even essential, performance attitudes because of its association with a decrease in emotional tension and increase in Joy.

Rita Carter noted in *The Human Brain Book* that according to research on facial expression and emotions there are six basic human emotions: surprise, anger, disgust, fear, happiness, and sadness.

I was struck that evolution has given us only one positive out of the six: happiness. I prefer to call this emotion Joy. I think of Joy as embracing a more full range of positive emotion than happiness. I experience Joy when I hear my wife laugh at the antics of our old cat Beanie, as well as when I am moved deeply hearing a fine orchestral performance of the Richard Strauss tone poem *Also Sprach Zarathustra*.

I have found that there is a precursor attitude to Joy. It is Appreciation (gratitude). After I appreciate something, I experience Joy. It can come in a wide range of magnitudes, from a little delta (quantum physics term for small change) to an overwhelming consciousness-saturating experience. For me, Joy is always preceded by the attitude of Appreciation, and invariably it brings life-affirming positive energy to my performance. Using ML-P concepts, the audience attitude of Appreciation invites the expansion of the Inner Performer's capacity to make creative choices. The presence of Appreciation within the performer facilitates the expansion toward the highly enjoyable state of peak performance. The interaction between the increased excellence of the performance and the Appreciation of the performer sets up a creative positive feedback loop, which moves the performer and the performance toward a state of oneness, which is peak performance.

Occasionally I hear the lament, "Oh, if I could just be more happy with my performance." The Perfectionist qualification is that the performance must be perfect *before* the performer gives self-permission to experience Joy. This is an example of self-defeating, product thinking. Masterful Life-Performance would say that in order to invite the Joy embedded in every performance, you first choose to appreciate your performance. You do it on a thought-by-thought basis, because anytime you think about your performance, you are performing.

I've included a story illustrating Appreciation coupled with Joy. Sometimes I find this divine pair in the most unlikely places. En "Joy,"

Ron

Christmas Story

You would remember his appearance for the same reasons I do, the pronounced scar across the right cheek of his fresh adolescent face and his steady inquiring hazel eyes. My client, a tall muscular seventeen-year-old, had been discharged after spending the sixteenth year of his life in prison. He was as proud as he could be about getting his own one-room apartment. Over the phone his excitement was obvious.

"Hey Ron, remember me, Charles?"

I recognized the voice right away. "Hey Charles, how are you?"

"I'm out now, and I can't believe it. They gave me my own place. I'll show it to you. How about picking me up? I'm over at the court-house."

"Charles, it's great you're out. Give me a few minutes. I'll meet you at the front entrance."

Having counseled him before his incarceration, I was familiar with stories of his childhood. I recalled his pride in telling me that at age ten his life circumstances had required him to forage in the forest, successfully finding food in the wild for himself and his four-year-old sister.

On the way over, my eye caught sight of Christmas wreaths, all lined up, hanging on the outside wall of the local nursery. I stopped and bought a small plain wreath. When he got in my truck, I gave him a welcoming smile and handed the wreath to him.

"Thanks Ron. You didn't have to do that."

"Just a little house-warmer, Charles. Congratulations. Merry Christmas."

He began by telling me about his first day in prison. As I listened, I reflected on the context of his story, his neglect-saturated early childhood, his age at entering prison, his fierce will to survive, and his matter-of-fact narrative style. It was like listening to a circuit judge reciting the facts of a legal brief.

"After they strip-searched me, they put me in a little cell with two other guys. There was a tiny window up high in the back. The place smelled. I hated the sound of that cell door clanging shut behind me. Then this big dude got in my face and told me to take off my shoes. He said they were his. Then he pointed to the lower bunk. He said it was the other guy's. He said the top one was his, and I would sleep on the floor.

I dropped him right there. While he was on the floor, bleeding, I told him the shoes and the top bunk were mine. He could sleep on the floor. I told him if he fucked with me again, he wouldn't be this lucky. From then on I watched my back. I got thirty days in the hole for that incident. Last year I spent a lot of time in the hole. I tricked the doctor into giving me more and more sleep meds. I slept while the other guys in solitary screamed."

We climbed the old narrow staircase to the third floor. Entering the dingy room, lit by a single bare bulb hanging from the ceiling, I noticed some foil-covered packets of tea on the card table, the only piece of furniture in the room. I walked over to a large dirty picture window, to check out his view. From his vantage point he had a panorama of the old granite-veneered Vermont town. Lots of sunshine hit the window when the winter clouds allowed. With the most relaxed expression I'd ever seen on him, he looked across the room at me and said, "What I look forward to the most is seeing the sunshine come through that big window in the morning, and not having to watch my back 24/7."

His gratitude pulled me right in. This kid's message was simple and powerful. Thanks for the sunshine. Thanks for the personal safety. Thanks for a place I can call my own.

He hung his wreath on the wall right away. With a Charles smile of under-stated appreciation, he scooped up a handful of tea packets, his only means of reciprocating, and handed them to me. As I looked more closely, an array of my own emotions surfaced. He had given me a handful of condoms, flavored condoms: candy cane, chocolate, strawberry.

"You can get more for free anytime you want. There's a big basket of them in the men's room on the third floor of the courthouse, down the hall from Probation and Parole."

Ever-so-slightly shaking my head in humored disbelief, I thanked him.

LETTER 39

Ron,

Quite a guy, that Charles. Really just a kid. And having gone through all that. I bet he appreciated your kind attention. It must be rare in his world. Must be so refreshing, for someone like you to come along and treat him with kindness and dignity.

So I guess that's it for your list of seven unconditional attitudes. I kind of wish there were more. Glad you ended with Appreciation though. Coming from the Perfectionist's world, I think the two that stood out the most were Forgiveness (it's next to impossible for me to forgive myself for making errors) and Appreciation. I appreciate what others do. But as for me, I slip so easily back into the ol' double standard. But if it's like you said, and Forgiveness is the process, that really increases my curiosity about using it. Even with myself.

Also, I like the pairing of Appreciation and Joy. And I especially liked the emphasis on how Appreciation can be chosen and that it can invite positive energy into my performances.

I would like to get back to the question I brought up in my last letter: If it works well, why not do it all the time?

Evelyn

LETTER 40

Dear Evelyn,

Thanks for reminding me of your question: If it works so well, why not use it all the time?

When I first realized that the Real Audience was inside myself, and that I could perform to this loving audience of my own choosing, my trumpet performance improved dramatically. Also, at that time I quizzed myself with the same question: Why not use the process all the time? What is preventing me from using a process that has shown itself to be so beneficial?

I started assembling my answer with the obvious.

ML-P was a new way of being. I was used to the old way, beating myself into perfection, rather than loving myself into excellence. I was a creature of habit. I was well practiced in my old ways, and carefully taught, as the song in *South Pacific* goes. I slipped into my old ways when I stopped paying attention to my new process, and especially when the performance challenges intensified.

After many years in the role of a therapist, I have added another explanation. I have worked with people who have experienced abuse in many forms and to many degrees. Abuse creates habitual patterns of thought, emotion, and behavior, resulting in reactive views of the world, biased views of others, and a biased sense of self. Abuse can create response patterns described by psychologists as learned helplessness, in which negative attitudes, emotions and interpretations of circumstance keep a person stuck in unproductive behavioral patterns. In Masterful Life-Performance language, this is the condition in which my Internal Performer does not make choices (its primary function!) because I believe I cannot. I have learned that I am helpless. The choice-making part of my performance personality shrinks. It metaphorically goes back into its cave and does not come out to play. This condition creates an unproductive stuck state, the opposite of Flow.

Abuse, in whatever forms I have experienced, has taught me two basic lies. The first is that I am not free to exercise choice-full creative responses to challenging circumstances. The second is that I am not strong enough to handle the consequences of my choices. The legacy of abuse is the perpetuation of these cruel, self-inhibiting myths.

I believe that abuse can come to us in many forms, from many sources, and in many degrees. A social culture that believes in and practices punishment is propagating abuse. A family system that castigates or abandons its members is setting up its next generation to practice abusive patterns. Those who believe in and practice Perfectionism propagate a form of self-abuse.

For me, the great challenge is to accept this truth, and focus my resources on increasing life-affirming practices. I believe ML-P is one such practice.

Masterful Life-Performance holds that, as long as our consciousness is intact, we are free to exercise choice, and that the first step in any conscious creative performance is to choose our Internal Audience. This can be the stepping-off place, the genesis of creative performance.

It is my observation that the cruel legacy of abuse, in all its forms and degrees, eventually yields to the practice of choosing and using loving attitude toward self.

The way to maintain loving attitude toward self is to practice the presence of one's Ideal Internal Audience Cue, thereby intentionally inviting the life-affirming attitudes associated with the Cue. Another closely related choice can be helpful as well. This choice has to do with the Social Intent for doing the performance.

It is this Social Intent, and its effect on performance, that is the next area I would like to explore with you. It is an important part of ML-P, and has a profound role to play in reducing harmful emotional tension.

Ron

Dear Ron,

So you are saying that once I experience a positive change in my performance using ML-P, it is my choice as to whether I use it again. It is also my choice as to how often I use it and in what circumstances I use it.

I like your approach. You are not telling me to use it. You leave all the decisions up to me. Remember, I'm very interested in what you say, but I don't have your degree of experience using it, or your passion for the process yet.

I get the carefully taught part of what you said. I think, for better or worse, we are all carefully taught.

Your thoughts on the legacy of abuse also resonated with me. Perfectionist patterns of thought and behavior can be quite self-abusive. I don't have to look too far outside or inside myself to find examples of that. Cruel isn't too strong a word for these patterns.

Thanks for being clear about how to use ML-P. You make it sound so easy to prime myself to get started on a task or meet a challenge. Just choose a helpful Cue, and reflect on the Cue until the helpful attitudes take over. Then I'm off and running. It sounds so simple, but I think it takes practice. Maybe lots of practice.

And we're back on the subject of reducing harmful excessive anxiety. Right back where we started, and back where my interest gets fired up.

I'm all ears about what you have to say as to how my Social Intent affects my nerves in social situations.

Evelyn

LETTER 42

Dear Evelyn,

We are in agreement about the simplicity of the ML-P process. And also that simplicity does not equal ease or fluency. Yes, it takes practice for ML-P to become one's predominant approach to performance, and for ML-P to become a helpful tool in the management of performance anxiety. As for me, it's worth the effort. For others, the effort and payoff may be different. And there we are, back to individual choice and individual life experience.

Indeed, I will talk about this last component of the Masterful Life-Performance process, the effect of Social Intent on one's performance. Alfred Adler's theoretical contributions to the field of social psychology have had a strong influence on my own work. Adler developed what he called Individual Psychology, and the cornerstone of this psychology is Social Interest (Gemeinschaftsgefül). Social Interest has to do with the social orientation of an individual, the person's sense of community with others, as contrasted with one's private self-interests and concerns.

As you know, my graduate work was done at the Alfred Adler Graduate School in Minnesota. There it was mentioned that Alfred Adler believed a person's emotional wellbeing was dependent on their degree of Social Interest, and that one could not have too much of it. Part of Social Interest has to do with a person's Social Intent. Does the person interact with the intent to *give* to others, or is it rather to *get* from others? I think of a Social Interest orientation as one characterized by the intent to raise the quality of life for others. The deliberate choice of social intention is thus to enhance the life of another person, to *give* to them.

A section of my Master's thesis researched the relationship between stage fright and Social Interest. In 1993, I tested 74 musicians at the MacPhail Center for Music in Minneapolis. One of the results showed a significant correlation between stage fright and Social Interest. Statistically, the *givers* (those with higher Social Interest) experienced significantly less stage fright than the *getters* (those with lower Social Interest). Those who saw their performance as a gift, and their social purpose as delivering the gift, experienced significantly less performance anxiety.

The results showed that up to 16% of the participants' stage fright was influenced by their social orientation. I'm sure you will agree that, when you are in an anxiety-prompting situation, 16% of your anxiety is significant. It is for me, when I am out on stage with a delicate, difficult trumpet part to be executed. Even as I face the everyday challenges of daily living, I can reframe what I am doing as a gift for others, and invite a reduction of excess anxiety.

Again, the process is elegantly simple. In order to invite a reduction of emotional tension (anxiety), mentally reframe your performance as a gift, and reframe your *entire* Social Intent (the social reason for the performance) as simply to deliver the gift.

Evelyn, in light of your own life experience, please let me know if this part of ML-P makes sense to you.

Ron

LETTER 43

Dear Ron,

Your last letter made lots of sense. Giving to others has always been easier for me than trying to get something from them. Intuitively, it just makes sense. I found interest in your research results too. Especially that a performer's Social Intent would be so important a factor in reducing anxiety.

Also I don't have any trouble accepting that social contribution is important for emotional wellbeing. I'm happiest when I'm giving, and when my intent is to benefit others. I think Adler was onto something with his emphasis on the importance of Social Interest. I don't think I could do my surgical work if I didn't believe that I was giving my patients the best chance for a better life, and in some cases life itself.

Now I would like to take my time and review all your letters.

During the time we have corresponded, I have noticed a general lessening of emotional tension. I'm easier on myself, and it feels good. I'm more forgiving, and more self-assured. I'm starting to see myself through the eyes of my Cue, and little islands of calm joy are poking holes in my anxiety. My relationships, both with myself and others, have improved, as has the way I feel about my work. Thank you for your insights, and mostly for your caring. I intend to continue exploring ML-P at my own pace. Also, I plan to keep a journal. I'll share my findings with you, if you'd like.

Your Grateful Friend,

Evelyn

LETTER 44

Dear Evelyn,

It's been wonderful sharing the Masterful Life-Performance process with you, and receiving your astute reactions and comments. I definitely want to keep the conversation going, and will welcome discussing your future performance insights and experiences. The journal sounds like a great way to go forward.

Since this is the last letter for a while, I am going to include a summary of the Masterful Life-Performance process, along with a story illustrating how I used it in an actual concert performance. I've also included an additional story, the merits of which I'll leave to your judgment.

- The intent of Masterful Life-Performance is to empower people to experience peak performance in any chosen area of their lives, and to experience increased technical excellence, social contribution, and inner wellbeing by alleviating performance anxiety.
- It works on the principle that our behaviors, as well as our thought processes, can be conceptualized as performances, and as such are highly responsive to that ever-present *Inner Audience* which we associate with any particular performance activity.
- ML-P holds that a helpful *Inner Audience* can be consciously chosen to replace a critical and judgmental *Inner Audience* using a visual and/or audio *Cue*, and that the constellation of attitudes associated with the *Cue* is a primary determiner of the quality of the performance and the Joy experienced as we perform. In ML-P we perform to the *Inner Audience* using the chosen *Cue*.
- A pillar ML-P concept is that the constellation of attitudes associated with the chosen Cue, is the *Real Audience,* the primary source of creative energy for actualizing the performance.
- ML-P is a love-based process in that the *Ideal Inner Audience is a constellation of unconditionally loving attitudes.* A primary

goal of ML-P is to invite an increase in excellence *(Excellism),* acknowledging that real life performance has error. This is in contrast to the pursuit of perfection *(Perfectionism),* which is seen as a fear-based philosophy which has as its primary goal the elimination of error.

- Another pillar ML-P concept is that the *Social Intent* of the performer, the degree to which we intend to give to others through our performance, is a primary determiner of the quality and Joy of our performance as well. When the *Social Intent* of the performance is to raise the quality of life for others, the performer experiences emotional regulation such that damaging excess emotional tension is reduced. In ML-P our *social intent* is to perform *for* others.

- ML-P holds that technical skill development is a necessary precursor for excellence in performance. Technical skill development is critical to actualizing excellence in performance.

In summary, when our Inner Audience is encouraging, our Social Intent is to give, and our technical skills and resources are functional, we tend to invite, and may even experience, peak performance.

Evelyn, please contact me anytime you want to talk about performance and/or performance anxiety. I have thoroughly enjoyed our exchange of letters, and look forward to sharing future performance experiences, observations and ideas anytime.

Cheers,

Ron

The Trumpet Shall Sound

Just now, right in the middle of this *Messiah* concert, the musical gift was delivered. We, and all present in this large church, heard it in the final chord of *The Trumpet Shall Sound*. There it was, full of surprise in its balanced tonal richness. Like the last flash of a full-spectrum sunset presenting its primary color, the chord revealed a predominant voice, the triumphant timbre of the trumpet.

Ron, our trumpeter, would say that it was our spirit-voice moving through him during the whole of Handel's inspired bass and trumpet duet.

And who are we? The ancient Greeks would call us muses. We are those who make Ron's artistry possible. We give him both technical direction and emotional sanctuary from the unbearably heavy burden of Perfectionism, the harbinger of excess anxiety. We free him to embrace his pursuit of excellence.

We are the influences of his teachers as well as his colleague-performers. We give him clarity in his artistic goals and standards in the moment. Also, we are the tonal, verbal and visual Cues he chooses to prompt his internal attitudes, the constellation of which he considers his Real Audience. These unconditional loving attitudes allow him to take carefully considered and wholehearted risks. And we are those sitting out in the concert hall for whom he plays tonight, his beloved, those he believes will be specifically benefitted by his performance gift.

Throughout the intense preparation period, as well as tonight's performance, he has mindfully chosen to invite our presence. For him, performance and thinking about a particular performance are one and the same. Habitually, he invites us into his process through his meditation. For him performance is a continuous, seamless, and primarily internal process. Holding this view throughout his preparation, Ron has internally performed the trumpet part to *Messiah* hundreds of times in his mind as well as in his practice room.

Tonight Ron's performance attitudes are being cued by a wallet-sized photocopy of Kahlil Gibran's sketch of the face of Jesus, *Good Friday,* which he visualizes throughout his performance. The curiosity, empathy and forgiveness generated by this discipline contribute to the dissolving of Ron's anxiety sufficiently to allow him to express freely and enter the peak performance state of Flow. Tonight he experienced Flow, the peak-performing state in which he and his performance were one.

Folded into his performance process is the clear Social Intent to deliver it as a gift to his friend Barbara. She was diagnosed with breast cancer yesterday, and is awaiting an additional biopsy report. When Barbara was told that Ron was going to play *The Trumpet Shall Sound*, she was happy and excited to attend the concert. The totality of Ron's social reason to perform is to give Barbara a few minutes of relief from her cancer concerns. Before the performance he positioned his music stand so that a line of sight two inches to the left of the stand would reveal Barbara's face as she listened far out in the hall. As he played the last note, Barbara's eyes were closed and a peaceful smile shone on her face. He could see that the gift had been received.

Image Reproduction Patricia Lyon-Surrey Fine Art Photography

Messiah

Performing Handel's *Messiah* a few years ago with the Vermont Philharmonic brought to mind a former memorable performance in Santa Barbara at the annual *Messiah* Sing-Along. I had just come from a Korean picnic where I had eaten spicy kim chee, and the other trumpeter had eaten garlic steak for lunch.

As we thundered in on our first trumpet entrance, the jubilant chorus *Glory to God*, the second-violin section seated just in front of us, collapsed in a domino effect, each player bending over at the waist, perfectly choreographed. With their heads simultaneously turned back towards us, they whispered in a loud unison, "What *IS* That?!"

God has rarely been glorified on such an ill wind.

Acknowledgements

It's taken a strong social web of support to write and produce this book. My primary support has come from my wife, Maggie. She listened with care, consummate skill, and loving kindness to all the many drafts of the letters and stories. She was my writing teacher and my initial editor. She provided unconditional loving attitude all along the way.

This book is intended to be a legacy for my family: my daughters Kirsten, Elizabeth, Sylvia, and Elise; my grandchildren Aaron, Kai, Kent and Ashley; my niece Shauna and my nephew Steve; my grandnieces and grandnephews Hannah, Caroline, Walker, and Logan. My hope is that each will share my belief that love is always present and that it is the great motivator of creative living.

The book is full of life stories of people with whom I have lived and worked. It has been a great privilege to see them meeting their challenges, giving me a perspective filled with wonder and gratitude. I hope this is reflected in my writing.

I've had a dream team of teachers beginning with my mother Evelyn, my father Ronald, and my brother Richard.

My passion for trumpet performance was shaped by four virtuosos: William Peron, William Vacchiano, Charles Schlueter, and Lloyd Geisler.

What I learned about performance from Eloise Ristad is written indelibly on my memory.

Thanks to Sherry Lowry, wise visionary and maven, who opened my eyes to the broad application of ML-P.

It is said that the teacher appears when the student is ready. The timing of Herbert Laube, Ph.D. of the Alfred Adler Graduate School, and Marshall Rosenberg, Ph.D. of The Center for Nonviolent Communication, was impeccable.

My thanks go to Gary Clark and The Vermont Studio Center for awarding me a life-changing week at the Center, where I discovered my writer's voice, and learned how to write a sentence.

Special thanks go to Susan Forter Browne, who brainstormed with me on what to name this approach, and who suggested "Masterful Life-Performance."

Special thanks go to Melissa Perley for her comment, "You need to call the book *On Cue*."

Maggie's writing workshop has provided a long-term supportive community of writers. Jane Bryant's encouraging, "Just do it." Justine O'Keefe's, "Ron, you have a whale by the tail." Lyn Kasvinsky's, "Remember, the author has the last word." I learned from Paul Mascitti not to use clichés, because they render one's writing dead as a doornail. Priscilla Daggett showed me when my writing contained redundancies, which constitute the repetition of phrases which don't need repetition or repeated clarification. She was dynamite with dangling modifiers too. Erik Esselstyn's Hubble telescopic mind could track the slightest trace of my tangential sense of humor. It's great when you can just read your writing, and know that it will be held by gentle keen minds. Julia Gresser and Sarah Houston both qualify.

My thanks go to those who read and commented on the various drafts: Kirsten Loiseaux-Purcell, Jane Bryant, Kathryn Davis, Patricia Fontaine, Anne Mixer, Tom Kyle, Peter Rousmaniere, Ron Sarquiz, Linda Schutz, Gail Kilkelly, Elizabeth Wilcox, Maria Kelley, Rosemary Hart, Nancy Ball.

Jean Gibran's responsiveness to my inquiries about Kahil Gibran's sketch of the face of Jesus, *Good Friday*, was a heartening surprise.

It has been a joy working with Patricia Lyon-Surrey, whose photography has contributed profoundly to this work. She has the eye of an artist. I don't know how many times I said "Wow!" when she presented her work to me.

Judging by the amount of red ink on the draft coming back from my editor Josie Masterson-Glen, her contribution was significant. However, her contribution went far beyond technical expertise. The uplift I felt from her heartfelt response to the message of the book was truly inspiring.

Graphic Designer Annie Clark has the uncanny ability to play with material until it emerges as a work of art. Lucky me, to have found Annie.

Thanks to the unmentioned many who also arrived as if on cue.

R.E.T.

May 2014

Bibliography

LETTER 4:
Rosenberg, Marshall. *Nonviolent Communication, A Language of Life, Second Edition*. Encinitas, California: PuddleDancer Press Book, 2003.

LETTER 6:
Ristad, Eloise. *A Soprano On Her Head, Right-Side-Up Reflections on Life and Other Performances*. Moab, Utah: Real People Press, 1982.

LETTER 11:
Emmons, Robert A. *Thanks!, How Practicing Gratitude Can Make You Happier*. New York: Houghton Mifflin Company, 2008.

LETTER 20:
Armstrong, Louis. *Satchmo, My Life in New Orleans*. New York: Signet, 1955.

Eaton, Jeanette. *Trumpeter's Tale, The Story of Young Louis Armstrong*. New York: William Morrow & Company, 1955.

Frankl, Viktor. *Man's Search for Meaning*. London: Rider, 2008. Reprinted by permission of The Random House Group Ltd., London and Beacon Press, Boston.

LETTER 35:
Beaufort, M. and Lawrence, Brother. *The Practice of the Presence of God*. Oxford, England: Oneworld, 2013.

LETTER 38:
Carter, Rita, et al. *The Human Brain Book*. New York: DK Adult, 2009.

LETTER 42:
Adler, Alfred. *Superiority and Social Interest, Third Revised Edition*. New York: W.W. Norton & Company, 1964.

PHOTO CREDITS

Cover Photo: *Autumn in Black & White,* Patricia Lyon-Surrey Fine Art Photography.

Letter 6: *Purple Fairy Boots,* Olson, Christine, ed. *Songs for Eloise.* Self Published, Northampton, Mass., Image Reproduction Patricia Lyon-Surrey Fine Art Photography.

Letter 8: *A Gift,* Patricia Lyon-Surrey Fine Art Photography.
No Big Deal, Patricia Lyon-Surrey Fine Art Photography.

Letter 12: *Learnin' to Drive,* Patricia Lyon-Surrey Fine Art Photography.

Letter 18: *Dog Story,* Image Reproduction Patricia Lyon-Surrey Fine Art Photography.
Grampa Red, Patricia Lyon-Surrey Fine Art Photography.
Mom, Carnegie Hall New York NY, Photo Copyright: Jeff Goldberg/Esto.
Speaking in Tongues, Patricia Lyon-Surrey Fine Art Photography.

Letter 20: *Satchmo,* Jack Bradley publicity photograph of Louis Armstrong in 1961. Courtesy of the Louis Armstrong House Museum.
The Bird, Patricia Lyon-Surrey Fine Art Photography.

Letter 22: *Ferrari Mind,* Patricia Lyon-Surrey Fine Art Photography.

Letter 26: *Great Beginner,* Patricia Lyon-Surrey Fine Art Photography.
Thad, Patricia Lyon-Surrey Fine Art Photography.

Letter 28: *Little League,* Patricia Lyon-Surrey Fine Art Photography.

Letter 30: *No,* Image Reproduction Patricia Lyon-Surrey Fine Art Photography.
Charlie, Image Reproduction Patricia Lyon-Surrey Fine Art Photography.

Letter 32: *Escape,* Patricia Lyon-Surrey Fine Art Photography.
Casino, Patricia Lyon-Surrey Fine Art Photography.

Letter 34: *Swedish Fish,* Patricia Lyon-Surrey Fine Art Photography.
Harold, Patricia Lyon-Surrey Fine Art Photography.
A Philosophical Conversation, Patricia Lyon-Surrey Fine Art Photography.

Letter 36: *Brother Lawrence,* Patricia Lyon-Surrey Fine Art Photography.
Nursing Home, Patricia Lyon-Surrey Fine Art Photography.
Cuz, Image Reproduction Patricia Lyon-Surrey Fine Art Photography.

Letter 38: *Christmas Story,* Patricia Lyon-Surrey Fine Art Photography.

Letter 44: *Good Friday: A Study.* A pencil drawing by Kahil Gibran (Harvard University Library). Image Reproduction Patricia Lyon-Surrey Fine Art Photography.

RON Thompson is a Psychologist-Master in private practice in
Montpelier, Vermont. His primary clinical emphasis is to increase
empathic understanding and reduce destructive anxiety within
individuals, couples, and families. During his twenty years as a
clinician he has worked with people representing a wide variety of
mental health challenges, including performance anxiety, depression,
generalized anxiety, couples and family conflict, interpersonal communication skill deficits, abuse issues, and anxiety secondary to autism.

Drawing from this, and coupled with his life-long involvement
with classical music, he has developed a psychology of peak

performance called Masterful Life-Performance, the principles and practice of which have been applied to a wide range of roles and settings. These include stage drama, music auditions and concerts, public speaking, athletics, preparation for surgery, creative writing, marital intimacy issues, professional and academic test taking, and the performance of daily living.

Ron has educational/professional backgrounds in three disciplines: symphonic trumpet performance (Juilliard, National Symphony of Washington D.C.); electrical engineering (University of California Santa Barbara, General Motors Corporation); and counseling psychology (Alfred Adler Graduate School, Minnesota, Vermont Licensed Psychologist-Master).

Pictured with Ron is his wife Maggie, who is a mother, grandmother, homemaker, writing teacher, memoirist, artist, musician, calligrapher, quilter, and bright light in Ron's life.

PATRICIA Lyon-Surrey is an artist specializing in fine art photography. She lives and works in Vermont and her photographs have been widely exhibited. Current interests include abstract photography, surreal montage and photographic triptychs.

(Website: patricialyonsurrey.com)

17765340R00100

Made in the USA
Middletown, DE
08 February 2015